I0146140

SOMEWHAT CENTRIST, SLIGHTLY SEXIST SEASONAL RANTS

Somewhat Centrist, Slightly Sexist Seasonal Rants

Musings from the Alto Section

JINNY BATTERSON

Contents

Dedication

for Sally, Bruce, Jim V. and Jim B., who've helped me make some sense of my past and present

and

for Jason, Kelly, Scott, Morgan, Parker B., Mylee, Ada, Brooks, Parker S., and Kenley, who help keep me hopeful about a more humane, more resilient future.

copyright Jinny Batterson, 2023

Introduction

The essays in this collection appeared in earlier form on my blog, jinnyoccasionalpoems. I've adjusted some to make them more timely, changed others to make them more timeless. I've created a structure to hold the twenty-four pieces included here.

I don't agree with claims that the United States of America is currently unremittingly polarized politically. My personal experience tends more toward a moving, moveable center, hence the "somewhat centrist" tone of this collection.

Both nature and nurture have confirmed a feminine identity for me in this lifetime. I've had chances for motherhood and also the need for reliable, accessible contraception. I've experienced mild gender discrimination and also had access to tools for counteracting some of it. My viewpoint is "slightly sexist."

I am someone who relishes time outdoors. As I contemplated a structure for these essays, I selected two essays per month and tried to tie most essays to events or to seasonal changes in the Northern Hemisphere where I've spent most of my life. These are, to some extent, "seasonal" essays.

These are opinion pieces. They are not intended to be objective. Though I hope they are adequately researched and reasoned, they are still "rants."

The distaff side of my heritage was musically talented. My mother and my maternal grandmother each spent a large portion of their work lives teaching vocal or instrumental music. Both Mom and Granny nudged me further into music-making, as accompanist or performer. I'm grateful they did not try to make me into a soloist, a terrifying prospect. Still, my gift for providing a piano background or a harmony among other musicians was/is a wonderful outlet.

When I reached middle school, I began to experience "parts singing" in a school chorus. Two of my childhood girlfriends and I had earlier learned about singing in harmony while practicing rounds with our Girl Scout troop. Our middle school music teacher assigned us to "hold the line" of altos in our mixed-voice chorus, right next to the soprano section. Most singers, when first exposed to singing in parts, revert to the soprano or melody line, the part we've usually learned first or best. It takes some time and effort to train one's ear to hear the melody without following along. Maureen, Ann, and I could belt out the alto line consistently and loudly enough so that the other altos singing next to us would be less likely to veer back into singing soprano.

For the rest of my life so far, I've participated in school choruses, glee clubs, church choirs, community choruses. During times when I've lived outside the U.S., music has often provided a bridge between cultures. Though tonal systems differ from place to place, I've nearly always found some way to thrive as an "alto" in harmony with local melodies.

At some point during the 1990's, I attended a weekend workshop at which one of the speakers was a "cultural anthropologist" named Angeles Arrien. This petite woman explained that all the world's cultures contain four basic archetypes. Arrien's seminal book, *The Four-Fold Way*, describes these archetypes and their signal behaviors:

Leader—show up and choose to be present;
Healer—follow what has heart and meaning;
Visionary—tell the truth without blame or judgment;
Teacher—be open to outcome, but not attached to it.

At this juncture, our American culture can too often lack an adequate supply of any of these archetypes. We use all sorts of numbing and isolation strategies to avoid showing up; we frequently follow and focus on the heartless or meaningless; what truths we do tell are heavily blaming and judgmental; we want our desired outcome(s) to prevail at all costs.

As I've attempted to put Arrien's archetypes to use in my own life, I've found them to be both difficult and rewarding. In the essays that follow, I hope you'll get occasional glimpses of presence, of paying proper attention, of truth-telling without judgment, of non-attachment.

Enjoy! Hallelujah!

Chapter 1

Epiphany

"Connections are made slowly, sometimes they grow under-ground.
You cannot tell always by looking what is happening."
—Marge Piercy

Prior to 2021, the date January 6 was mostly known as Epiphany, the "Feast of the Three Kings," in the liturgical calendar of many Christian denominations. "Epiphany" has also come to mean any illuminating discovery, typically of some previously unknown good or truth. In many traditions, the Epiphany holiday celebrates the revelation of Jesus as a special child, sent to minister to everyone, visited and acknowledged by Magi from far away bearing gifts.

In 2021, January 6 became also a day of shame for American democracy. Whatever the eventual outcome of investigations into the event, the Capitol riot that day further damaged the reputation of the United States of America as a supposed example of functioning self-government. Around the anniversary of the riot, news about other issues can get temporarily shunted aside. To avoid getting overloaded, I turn off all media and go for a walk outside. I become aware of the lengthening of days and the beginnings of new life, whatever the weather.

In January, 2017, I took part in a different mass event, the January 21 "women's march global." That day, on the National Mall in Washington, D.C., half a million attendees, mostly women, converged for peaceful protests and speeches supporting women's rights, environmental responsibility, and a variety of other causes. In North Carolina, my home then, I participated in a hastily organized Raleigh event which drew about 17,000 people, twice the number that local organizers and police had planned for. Despite the large crowd, this event was also peaceful, with humor, flexibility, even camaraderie between some police officers and some marchers.

The size of the January 6, 2021 Washington, D.C. demonstration prior to the Capitol assault has been variously estimated at from several thousand to as many as 20,000. Not all participants in the rally were involved in the subsequent riot. According to an ongoing study by researchers at the University of Chicago Project on Security and Threats, of those arrested for their actions that day, 86% were male.

As someone comfortable with a female identity, if not with the restrictions a female identity has sometimes imposed, I'm both curious and concerned about the gender disparities of the 2017 and 2021 events. A half million mostly female demonstrators in Washington in 2017 managed a peaceful protest with no damage and no arrests, while a small fraction of that number of mostly male attendees in 2021 resulted in multiple deaths, an estimated $2.7 million in damage to the U.S. Capitol, and nearly a thousand arrests so far.

Women who helped organize the 2017 events have not stopped working, but have sometimes gotten less visible. We have turned to other avenues in our attempts to support meaningful change. The focus is both local and global. We highlight the efforts of women in the "global south," such as

Prime Minister of Barbados Mia Amor Mottley. In an address to the 2022 session of the U.N. General Assembly, this head of the government of a small island nation explained:

"Any attempt to deny that the climate crisis has man-made origins is an attempt to delude ourselves and to admit that we want to be accomplices in the continuing death and loss . . . that ensues to the people who are the victims of it."

Women (and men) in economically underdeveloped countries such as Barbados have contributed little to current global problems but are disproportionately impacted by them. Partly because of ongoing efforts such as Ms. Mottley's, in 2022 the COP27 global climate conference for the first time agreed to set up a "loss and damage fund" to help the most vulnerable countries adapt to increasingly disruptive climate change.

Wherever we live on our planet, it is true that disasters and conflicts disproportionately impact women.

Paying too much attention to the news can be disheartening. Going for a walk helps me regain perspective. I also find solace in some favorite lines of a favorite poet, Marge Piercy's "The Seven of Pentacles:"

"..[S]he is looking at her work growing away there
actively, thickly like grapevines or pole beans
as things grow in the real world, slowly enough. ...

Connections are made slowly, sometimes they grow underground.
You cannot tell always by looking what is happening."

It's my fervent wish that we can soon return to the pre-2021 celebrations of January 6, that we can continue the Magis' wisdom and celebrate the unique talents of each new child born. Among us are multiple children with the latent capacity to minister to our ailing world.

Jesus' ministry stressed compassion and inclusion. He modeled a true masculinity that did not require rioting and destruction. There is ample room nowadays for a masculinity that supports equal access to life's opportunities, that can be strong without bullying, that does not depend on vilifying an "other" to be validated.

Each of us, whatever our gender, can continue work on our own unique tasks in the global effort to reinforce the solidarity and acknowledge the mutual vulnerability we share on this planet with its over 8 billion temporary human guests. May we enter each new January with the openness for another epiphany.

Chapter 2

Reproductive Health

*"A person may choose to have an abortion until a fetus be-
comes viable, based on the right to privacy contained in the Due
Process Clause of the Fourteenth Amendment. Viability means
the ability to live outside the womb, which usually happens between 24 and 28 weeks after conception."*
—primary holding of the 7-2 Roe v. Wade U.S. Supreme
Court decision, January 22, 1973

Disagreements about the legal status of women and, as a
corollary, the legality of abortion, have existed for a very long
time. Abortion is a complex issue. Early in our country's history, abortion was not treated as a legal matter. Most women's
health care was provided informally by female relatives or by
midwives, many with expertise in herbal medicine. Then, over
the course of the 19th century, American abortion laws were
codified and made stricter, partly due to increasingly power-
ful lobbying by (mostly male) physicians. Starting in the late
1960's, the pendulum swung the other way and abortion laws
began to be liberalized. By the time the U.S. Supreme Court
in January, 1973 handed down its ruling removing restrictions
on early term abortions throughout the U.S. (Roe vs. Wade),

abortions were already legal under some circumstances in 30 of the 50 U.S. states. When the plaintiff called "Roe" began her suit in Texas in 1969 demanding the right to an abortion, state law there permitted abortions, but only to save the life of the mother.

For months leading up to the 2022 U.S. Supreme Court Dobbs decision, I dreaded its potential impact on our fractured body politic. As a post-menopausal woman, I was no longer directly impacted by the twists and turns of abortion rulings and legislation. During my fertile years, I'd been privileged to live in areas where reliable contraception was available and reproductive options were improving. I've been blessed with two healthy, much-wanted children and a long-term partner who helped provide both material and emotional support as we navigated the grand adventure of parenting. Still, I've paid some attention to the ongoing debates about "life" and "choice." I have younger friends who may be impacted by court decisions and legislation going forward. I have granddaughters.

In ideal cases, a developing fetus is the result of consensual sex between prospective adult parents. Ideally, once a woman's egg is fertilized, the resulting zygote begins to divide, then implants and thrives in utero throughout the pregnancy, which ends when a healthy mother delivers a healthy infant. However, many hazards exist between conception and birth— miscarriage, ectopic pregnancy, maternal health complications, lethal fetal abnormalities. The rate of spontaneous miscarriage is estimated at between 11 and 22 percent of confirmed pregnancies. It seems probable that over half of all pregnancies end even before pregnancy is confirmed.

Ideally, prospective parents are financially and emotionally ready to raise to adulthood any child they conceive. However, a study from the New England Journal of Medicine in 2011 found then that nearly half of pregnancies were either "unplanned" (27%) or "unwanted" (18%). Per their research, unintended pregnancy rates are highest among low-income women, women younger than 24, unmarried women cohabiting with a male partner, and women of color. Economic studies repeatedly link limiting access to contraception and/or abortion to increases in child poverty and crime.

In the years leading up to the Roe decision in the U.S., some states with less restrictive laws became "abortion magnets" for women in adjoining areas who needed the procedure. Abortions were, and still are, more readily available to women with the financial means to pay and to travel, even internationally, if necessary. In one high-profile case in 1962, a married pregnant woman from Arizona went to Sweden for an abortion after she learned that thalidomide, an ingredient in a medicine she'd taken early in her pregnancy, could cause severe birth defects. It turned out that the fetus she'd carried was badly deformed. Had it not been aborted, it would likely have died at birth.

Before Roe, many pregnant young women opted for rushed marriages, typically to the baby's father and typically before they showed many external signs of pregnancy. Another possibility was to obtain an illegal abortion or to attempt to self-abort. Either could have serious legal and health consequences. Estimates vary widely for the number of pre-Roe "stealth abortions" in the U.S., but such abortions did occur, along with related maternal injuries and deaths.

A different option was to have the child and then surrender the infant for adoption. As I tried to find a touchstone for considering the larger issues surrounding women's reproductive health, I came across a book about this option: Ann Fessler's 2006 study, *The Girls Who Went Away: The Hidden History of Women Who Surrendered Children for Adoption in the Decades Before Roe v. Wade*. Fessler first estimates the number of mothers who surrendered infants for adoption during the pre-Roe period 1945-1973—roughly 1.5 million, or an average of over 50,000 per year. Most of the young women who relinquished their infants had limited financial and emotional resources. They were under tremendous societal pressure to conform to the stereotype of the "good girl," one who presumably did not have sex and therefore could not get pregnant. Fessler, an adoptee herself, personalizes her statistics through individual oral histories of the experiences and trajectories of over a hundred of these mothers who were willing to be interviewed about their lives—before, during, and after their adoptive pregnancy.

The era of the 1950's and 60's had a severe double standard about the consequences of sexual activity for young men and young women, some of which persists. As Fessler remarks: "Hearing these women tell their stories today, one can't help but acknowledge the unfairness of calling them 'bad girls' and of the social scorn that was inflicted almost exclusively on them, and not on the young men with whom they had conceived." Through her interviewees, the author paints a vivid picture of the emotional shaming of young women who "got in trouble": "This was in that period of time when there wasn't much worse that a girl could do. They almost treated you like you had committed murder or something. —Toni"

Most girls who opted to complete their pregnancies outside marriage were sent to homes for unwed mothers to wait out the remaining months of their pregnancies, give birth, and almost immediately decide on the future of their newborn child. Most homes for unwed mothers in postwar America exerted pressure on their clients to relinquish their infants. Few young women were given any counseling about the sense of bereavement they might feel. For many, this has left lifetime scars: "Giving up my son was a seminal moment in my life. People will say, 'Get over it.' I can't tell you how many people say, 'Aren't you ever going to get over it?' Never. You never get over this. Men often go to the military and fight in wars and they never really get over what they see. This is like one of those huge tragedies in your life. That's how I look at it, as a tragedy. It's a tragedy because it didn't have to happen.—Maggie"

Shortly before the court's Dobbs decision was officially announced, I participated in a local demonstration in support of women's reproductive health. At the event, a lot of women in my 70+ age cohort expressed outrage at the prospect of having to fight the "coat hanger wars" all over again. In prior generations, too many women had died or suffered irreparable harm due to botched abortions, either from self-induced attempts or at poorly run illegal clinics. A bent coat hanger became a symbol of this carnage.

One demonstration sign that moved me was a simple one. On a piece of cardboard, it recorded a woman's name with her birth and death dates: 1907-1930. The great-niece who was marching in this woman's memory explained that her grandmother's married sister had become pregnant with her fifth child at the beginning of the Great Depression. Lacking resources to stretch beyond the children she'd already borne, the woman tried to self-abort. She died in the attempt. Per physician and researcher Christopher Tietze, there were 2,677 officially recorded abortion deaths in the U.S. in 1933. Starting in the 1940's, abortion deaths declined with the introduction of antibiotics and the increasing skill of those performing most abortions.

At many 2022 demonstrations across the U.S., younger women opted for variations on a "don't tread on me" theme, with a rattlesnake coiled inside a stylized uterus. There were also a good many signs comparing women's reproductive rights with gun rights: "America, where my body has fewer rights than an AR-15." Some signs advised, "Listen to black women."

What continues to non-plus me about the abortion debate in the U.S. is how much it compartmentalizes the period of gestation as somehow separate from the periods before and after a pregnancy. Although alternative pregnancy options in industrialized countries are becoming available, if hugely expensive, the vast majority of fetuses are the result of male/female intercourse. When we concentrate overmuch on the period of gestation and the sometimes conflicting legal rights of prospective mothers and their yet-to-be-born children, we too often short-circuit other needed efforts. We neglect effective measures that would reduce the incidence of unplanned or problem pregnancies in the first place. We fail to consider other measures that could enhance the lives of many children *after* their births.

Now that the Dobbs decision has changed the legal landscape surrounding abortion, I am doing my best to craft a forward-looking response. No legal decision regarding abortion will satisfy anyone completely. Abortions will continue being performed, whether legally or illegally. For now, an America in which every child is deeply wanted and loved, in which no mother dies from complications of pregnancy or delivery, in which each new human is born into a fully functional family and society, remains a distant dream.

I continue to hope that the distractive tactic of pitting us against each other about the period of gestation will prove less effective over time. Then, maybe, we'll be able to see beyond our differences on abortion to lessen the damage we are causing to the already born and to women not ready to bear additional children. Our faith, our gender, and our life circumstances can help us absorb the wisdom we will need to navigate post-Dobbs America. I continue to work for a society that concentrates less on what happens inside the womb and more on what happens in the world into which babies are born.

Chapter 3

Unacknowledged Cousins: Reimagining 'White' Womanhood

..."(N)o white woman reared in the South or perhaps anywhere else in this racist country, can find freedom as a woman until she deals in her own consciousness with the question of race."
—Anne McCarty Braden

At the inner city elementary school that my children attended, both were exposed early to black history, courtesy of a gifted third grade teacher who had them research and report on outstanding black authors, scientists, inventors, and civil rights activists. A little of my children's training has rubbed off on me. Each February, during Black History Month, I make an effort to read at least one relevant book. This year, I'm additionally writing to try to articulate my evolving understanding of the social construct of race.

My early upbringing stressed that I was "white," as opposed to a few "black" students who began when I was in fifth grade to attend the same Maryland public elementary school I did. Whiteness has benefited me in many ways. For much of my life, it also partially blinded me to the violence and discrimination historically visited on those who are "not white," some of which continues.

As I've aged, the whole notion of "whiteness" has become suspect. Much of the history I was earlier taught whitewashed the impact of enslavement and supported the myth of white supremacy, upholding both slavery and its more contemporary descendants—Jim Crow, mass incarceration, jingoism, xenophobia, disenfranchisement.

Partway through my work life, I spent a couple of years in a sub-Saharan African country as a junior member of a project supporting small-scale local consumer cooperatives. I noticed that my African colleagues and neighbors were generally darker skinned than most African-Americans I encountered while living in the United States. Once I returned to the U.S., I was advised by an African-American friend here that most people who self-identify as "black" in the U.S. have at least some "white" ancestry.

That got me to thinking. For much of my work life, I lived in central Virginia. The history I'd been taught in my youth idolized Thomas Jefferson among the founders of our republic—author of the Declaration of Independence and the Virginia Statute of Religious Freedom, Governor of Virginia, Ambassador to France, Secretary of State, President of the United States. Several times I made a pilgrimage to Jefferson's "retirement" home of Monticello just outside Charlottesville. Little of the story of Monticello as it was then told related to Jefferson's position as a slave holder. Over time, I began to read and learn more about the seamier side of a slavery-based economy. A few years ago, long after I'd left Virginia, an exhibit was mounted at Monticello describing the life of Sally Hemings. Although enslaved from birth, Hemings was likely the mother of several of Jefferson's children. The exact nature and complexity of the Jefferson-Hemings relationship remains controversial, but it's fairly well established that Hemings was a half-sister to Jefferson's white wife, Martha Skelton Jefferson, and that after Martha died, Jefferson and Hemings were involved in some sort of relationship for several decades.

Jefferson and other white men whose historical contributions I'd been taught to venerate may have engaged in sexual relations with enslaved black women, sometimes non-consensually. Might I have African-American cousins, the result of some of my white male ancestors impregnating their female slaves? It seems not entirely unlikely, though difficult to prove. An African-American friend recently explained that pre-Civil War genealogy for black families in the U.S. is hard to do, because record keeping was skimpy and generally did not include enough information to fully identify an enslaved person.

"Most of us can't go back further than a few generations," he said.

By contrast, the most thoroughly documented part of my northern European ancestry traces back a dozen generations to the Dutch tavern keeper who late in life resettled in what was then New Amsterdam. In a different branch of the family, one of my great-grandfathers was born in South Carolina in 1820 and later moved his family to Carthage, Mississippi. By the time my maternal grandfather was born there in 1869, the family were former slaveholders. I remember stories retold to me by my mother of how frightened her father had been as a small child to live in a house that also billeted federal troops.

The mythology long fed to "white" women, especially in the American South, was that white men were needed to "protect the sanctity of white womanhood." This viewpoint was hypocritical at best, often deliberately misleading and damaging. A white woman of my parents' generation, Anne Braden, whose work I recently discovered, put it eloquently. In the early 1950's, after reporting on the execution of a black man, Willie McGee, for the supposed rape of a white woman, Braden wrote:

"I believe that no white woman reared in the South or perhaps anywhere else in this racist country, can find freedom as a woman until she deals in her own consciousness with the question of race. We grow up little girls – absorbing a hundred stereotypes about ourselves and our role in life, our secondary position, our destiny to be a helpmate to a man or men. But we also grow up white – absorbing the stereotypes of race, the picture of ourselves as somehow privileged because of the color of our skin. The two mythologies become intertwined, and there is no way to free ourselves from one without dealing with the other."

The work of freeing ourselves of preconceptions and misconceptions is the work of all. However, in this era of divisiveness and disinformation, it is especially the work of "white" women. May we dedicate ourselves to continuing this work.

Chapter 4

Noticing a Tailwind

"Equality says we treat everyone the same, regardless of head-winds or tailwinds. Equity says we give people what they need to have the same access and opportunities as others, taking into account the headwinds they face, which may mean differential treatment for some groups."
—Dolly Chugh

In the wake of the 2020 police killing of George Floyd in Minneapolis and again after the fatal police beating of Tyre Nichols in Memphis in 2023, discussions and protests have erupted around issues of police brutality and systemic racism. Some legal reforms have been enacted, some changes in procedures have been put in place, but problems persist. I'm reminded of a long-ago vacation that included the first and only time when I viscerally experienced what it's like to have a tailwind or a headwind.

Back when my husband and I were younger and fitter, we sometimes planned bicycling vacations. An especially memorable one was a two-week jaunt to some then-isolated regions of eastern Canada during the 1990's. We reserved ten days' lodgings in the Canadian province of Prince Edward Island.

Partway through, we'd take a four day side trip to an even smaller, more remote set of islands further east—the Magdalen Islands, parts of Quebec province in the midst of the Gulf of St. Lawrence. Our initial setting out point was Charlottetown, PEI's capital and largest city. On our arrival, we wandered the town for a little while, getting oriented and marveling at the trilingual street signs (English, French, and Japanese). We learned that Charlottetown was a frequent honeymoon destination for Japanese brides who'd studied the "Anne of Green Gables" novels set in PEI in high school.

In late afternoon, we got a taxi to the bike rental agency where we'd reserved two appropriately sized bikes. We then pedaled off to our first night's lodging at a campground not far from town. For most succeeding nights, we stayed at small inns and B&B's about 30 miles apart, an easy day's ride in the generally flat or gently rolling terrain. Once we reached an eastern edge of PEI, we took a ferry from the small town of Souris to the even less populous Magdalens, known in French as Îles de la Madeleine. We'd reserved three nights' lodging near the ferry terminus and one on an island further north, connected to the main island by a narrow causeway.

After our first night's stay near the ferry and a plentiful breakfast, we pedaled off northward. We cruised easily along, spotting plovers and other shore birds as we went. The paved, rock-lined causeway was barely two car widths across. There was very little traffic. We reached our north island destination mid-afternoon. Our host was a dedicated birder. He gave us hints about when and where to get the best views of shore birds. Our accommodations were simple but ample. The sunset and star views were unsurpassed. The following morning, after another plentiful breakfast, we headed south, back the way we'd come.

Pedaling along the causeway this time felt as if we were propelling our bikes through a slick of molasses. On our way north, we'd been oblivious to a substantial tailwind. The wind had not shifted. Our return trip took us straight into a significant headwind. It was well into evening when we reached our third night's stay.

I cannot fully know what it is like to be a black person in the United States of America. The highly publicized murders of George Floyd and Tyre Nichols by police are just two instances of the unequal enforcement of laws and of codes of conduct based on race. Though I've studied about the traumas of slavery, Jim Crow, and mass incarceration, though I've had friends of color share a few of their individual stories with me, being non-white is not part of my lived experience.

Social psychologist Dolly Chugh and her colleagues have done lots of research into subconscious bias. They've learned that, because the volume of sensory impressions we're constantly bombarded with is beyond our conscious processing capacity, many of our responses are based on factors outside our conscious awareness. Unless we train ourselves to pause before reacting, we are likely to prejudge some people favorably, to respond to others unfavorably, without even knowing we are doing so. We are likely to remain ignorant of the tailwinds or headwinds that have helped shape our respective realities.

I'm often ignorant of the tailwinds that ease my life's journey. Experiencing bicycling into a headwind may be the closest I've come to knowing in my body what it can feel like to be "living while black" in today's America. Both in my individual actions and in my civic life, I need to become more aware of the tailwinds I've sometimes benefited from. I need to catch myself more often when I've made racist, sexist, classist or other "othering" assumptions. I need to recognize my errors, apologize when appropriate, then forgive myself and keep trying. With practice and effort, I can get better at helping make the headwinds buffeting others less severe.

Chapter 5

The Durability of Sisterhood

"A sister is like yourself in a different movie, a movie that stars you in a different life." —Deborah Tannen

One recent year, I attended three "women mostly" events in quick succession—an NAACP breakfast fundraiser and celebration of that group's North Carolina mother/woman of the year, the annual meeting of our local chapter of the League of Women Voters, and the 50th reunion of my class from Randolph College in Lynchburg, Virginia. At each event, there were a few men, as official escorts, unofficial companions, or male affiliates, but the focus was mainly on us women. I'd forgotten how good it can feel to be in sisterhood.

The NC NAACP celebration was the first formal NAACP event I'd attended in North Carolina. The venue was a Raleigh church. The event was held on a Saturday morning. Contestants and their supporters came from nearly twenty NAACP chapters throughout North Carolina. Because of another appointment, I missed the delayed keynote talk by Cheri Beasley, then Chief Justice of the North Carolina Supreme Court. Over the part of the event I did attend, I learned that the NAACP has been holding such annual celebrations since the 1950's.

The LWV Wake County annual meeting was held on a week-night at the faculty club of N.C. State University. There was a catered supper and a cash bar. I knew some "old stalwarts," but was pleased to notice younger faces new to me. The event was tightly scheduled. The business at hand—election of new officers, committee reports, financial updates—was quickly dispatched. Dinner conversations were pleasant and generally non-confrontational in this staunchly non-partisan organiza-tion. The Wake county LWV had been founded in 1920, the same year women got the right to vote in national elections. After a rocky period during the late 1930's and 1940's, the chapter reconstituted itself in 1950 and has been active ever since.

Then there was the Randolph reunion. I arrived near the beginning of the three-day weekend's festivities to a beautiful campus, mostly empty just after the close of the academic year. When I'd attended what was then Randolph-Macon Woman's College in the late 1960's, I was a good student, but certainly not a social standout. I sang in the glee club, but held no campus leadership positions and rarely attended campus-wide events. A foreign language major, I didn't contribute to campus publications. I wasn't a horsewoman or an athlete in any other sport. At graduation I felt that I'd made it through, but would likely not maintain much connection with the school.

As I found my reserved dorm room and settled in for the reunion, I wondered how fish-out-of-water I'd feel after fifty years away from this institution, founded in 1891 to promote the education of young women. Over its recent existence, it had evolved a lot. A decade or so earlier, faced with declining enrollment and difficulties attracting highly qualified women to a small, single-sex liberal arts school in the U.S. South, the trustees made a wrenching decision to become coeducational.

Alums of the most recent reunion class, returning five years after their graduation, were a rainbow mix of genders and backgrounds, though the school's student body had so far remained majority female.

More and more members of my former class filtered in. I was surprised at how many women I recognized and found connections with: still-active, still-engaged, still-vibrant septuagenarians whose energy was palpable. Of course we participated in some mutual bragging—further educational achievements, children, life partners, careers, travels, awards, humanitarian endeavors. Mostly, though, we shared stories based on the values we'd developed during a special time and place together in a supportive environment. Those values continued to illuminate our choices and preferences fifty years after graduation.

After lots of travel earlier in the year, I decided to skip a June Charlotte-area reunion of part of my biological family I'd become better acquainted with while living in North Carolina. I missed the chance to visit once more with three older sisters of my dad's generation, cousins related to me through my paternal grandmother's baby brother. Virginia, Betsy, and Judy were then in their 80's and 90's. They had lived long, fruitful lives. Through multiple challenges, they'd maintained a durable sisterhood.

My sister Sally didn't make it physically to her 80's or 90's. An ancillary casualty of the covid pandemic, Sally was done in by the additional stress of running a small farm and hospitality business during the worst of early pandemic lockdowns. She died in October, 2020. As nearly as we can tell, she suffered a heart attack early one morning while alone at her farmhouse. A friend found her body later that day. We grieve our loss, virtually or in person.

Sal was something of a gadfly, flaunting family "norms." She tried many different avenues for self-fulfillment before she found her calling. Eventually, in her 50's, she settled at the small farm our parents had purchased for a retirement that didn't pan out. Sal was contemplating her own retirement when the pandemic increased food insecurity in her area. Rather than scaling back as previously planned, she scaled up her food production efforts. During her final few years, she'd written about her farm experiences on a blog and in small booklets she self-published and sometimes distributed as holiday gifts.

Sally's legacy lives on in my gardening and writing efforts. Sometimes I can almost hear her advice about weeding carrots, or weeding extra words from an essay. I'm gradually learning that sisters can stick together, no matter what tries to come between us.

Chapter 6

Gardening as
Spiritual Practice

"Earth was given as a garden, cradle for humanity;
tree of life and tree of knowledge placed for our discovery..."
—UU Hymnal *Singing the Living Tradition*, #207

The faith tradition I am part of has multiple core principals we affirm, one being "respect for the interdependent web of all existence (of which we are a part)." As we humans confront a series of interlocking crises surrounding our global climate, one of the ways I attempt to show respect is by honing my skills as a lifelong gardener.

In extensive travels so far, I've had chances to observe and to roam in gorgeous gardens on five continents. I've tried my hand at small-scale gardening on three of them. For me, the time I spend in direct contact with the earth is partly a spiritual practice.

I began gardening in childhood, tutored by my ex-farmer father. One dry summer in Maryland in the mid-1950's, when I was about eight years old, I was designated Dad's garden assistant. It was my job, a couple of times each week, to haul water to the bell pepper plants in our hillside garden. I'd fill two small buckets at the nearest outdoor spigot and take them uphill, being careful not to slosh water over the sides. Dad had created a saucer-shaped surround for each plant, so the water would have more chances to soak in, rather than run off. I'd carefully, slowly, water each pepper. The plants made it through the summer, producing enough peppers to add to salads, and later to feature in some stuffed pepper meals as the weather got cooler.

When our family moved nearby to a larger house with more land, we had a bigger garden. My main contribution to this garden was eating its produce to nourish my rapidly growing teen body. We had sweet corn. Despite the predations of area raccoons, there was always enough for a few delicious corn-on-the-cob meals, plus some breakfast corn fritters with leftover kernels.

We also grew tomatoes, their red fruits a source of contention between human eaters and the local turtle population. Every year, some ripe tomatoes had substantial chunks eaten out of them. We learned to plant enough to feed both humans and turtles, with the added benefit that we kids could capture tomato-munching turtles as entrants to our neighborhood's traditional Fourth of July turtle race.

My first adult gardening came when my newish husband and I moved from a series of urban environments to Vermont. Our premature attempt to "return to the land" lasted only a couple of years, but it gave me a chance to appreciate a more northern climate. In Vermont, cool weather crops grew that would have withered in the heat of Maryland's summers—romaine lettuce, broccoli, and a strange shaped cabbage relative called kohlrabi. I harvested quite a few of these greenish globes. I learned to cook them as a side dish. Unfortunately, when I tried them on my in-laws during their initial visit to our "rural haven," kohlrabi turned out to be my father-in-law's least favorite vegetable. Dad B. had spent a boyhood summer with his mom and sisters as a tenant on a friend's Midwestern farm. They'd eaten an abundance of kohlrabi. I learned never to serve them to my father-in-law again.

Our subsequent move to Richmond, Virginia included an initial stint of apartment living. However, once we'd purchased an older house with a yard, I began another gardening odyssey. The first chore was removing the growth of wild clematis that had spread across the poorly tended back yard. Next came turning the hard soil, adding fertilizer, then deciding what to plant. Tomatoes for sure. Maybe some corn. Peas, carrots, scallions, onions, green beans, lima beans, eggplant, and, one year, potatoes. Richmond summers were too hot and steamy for most cooler weather veggies. Some years, the weather went from freezing to stifling in just a few weeks. My early harvests did little to nourish our growing family. However, digging, hoeing, and weeding in my small garden forestalled the escalation of many a family fight.

Partway through our Richmond lives, I took a "sabbatical," a two-year stint in a Peace-Corps-like program in sub-Saharan Africa. I lived at the edge of a United Nations housing complex along the eastern shore of Lake Tanganyika. The climate was different from anything I'd encountered before. This close to the equator, day length and temperatures barely changed during the year. The main weather pattern was the alternation between dry and wet seasons. From late May to September or October, it rarely rained at all. A smattering of planting began in advance of the short rainy season, typically from late September until mid-December, when there could be a harvest of sorts. A short dry season in late December and January provided several storm-free weeks. Then it was time to plant in earnest. The long rainy season from January to May was when most foodstuffs were grown—staples like manioc, corn, and beans. Herders also harvested fodder for the cattle and other ruminants, enough to last through the long dry season until pasturage again became available with the short rains. Tropical fruits and trees abounded—pineapple, banana, mango, guava, passionfruit, avocado. However, some temperate climate crops refused to thrive. An Italian neighbor tried vainly to coax apples or grapes into production. Apparently, cold weather was needed for them to fruit.

On trellises outside my kitchen door, I grew straggly beans and peas. They did little to replace the need for the town market, where my housekeeper bargained for most of our food. Local fare was delicious and relatively inexpensive. I learned enough about this densely populated, predominantly rural part of East Africa to realize that a diet based mostly on beans, corn, and manioc made more sense than the western meat-heavy diet I'd been accustomed to before.

Once back in Richmond, I refined my techniques and produced enough vegetables to reduce the carping from other family members about my "less-than-minimum-wage" work. They acknowledged, too, that gardening for me was therapy. A local move to a property with a huge yard containing a level, sunny spot perfect for vegetable gardening increased my productivity. I enriched the soil with compost and further increased our harvests. The year we put the house up for sale, I went all out in early spring planting. Maybe the well-ordered rows of lettuce, scallions and spinach encouraged the buyers, who were also avid gardeners.

The next year, my empty-nester husband and I lived in a desert in northwestern China. In pots on our apartment windowsill, I grew basil and a few regularly-watered greens. More substantial harvests were beyond me. Our several subsequent jaunts in China were either too brief or too busy to allow me to plant a real garden. The year I lived in the "garden province" of Sichuan, though, I reveled in the variety and abundance of produce available in local markets.

A dozen years ago, at a church music camp, I got my first exposure to a hymn about gardens:

"Earth was given as a garden, cradle for humanity;
  tree of life and tree of knowledge placed for our discovery.
  Here was home for all your creatures born of land and sky and sea;
  all created in your image, all to live in harmony."

My gardening adventures in varied locales up to then had led me to believe that:
—other critters will eat part of your harvest no matter how strenuously you try to protect it, so plant enough to be able to share a little
—people's tastes differ; forcing a despised vegetable on someone does not work
—not everything will grow everywhere, but at least something will grow almost anywhere
—each gardening season is different, even in the same plot

My most recent move has been a late-life relocation nearer to some of my extended family in southern California. The climate here is "Mediterranean." We have long, increasingly hot dry seasons. If we are lucky, we get enough cool weather rains to green the hills in January and February. I have a small rented plot in a local community garden. Fellow gardeners coach me on water conservation techniques, on low-water plants, on organic methods for dealing with garden pests. Different gardeners come with different geographical and ethnic backgrounds, so we try a wide variety of plants, from tomatoes and zucchini to artichokes, bitter melon and dragonfruit.

This latest community garden is generally a joyous, peaceful place. We try to figure out what "wants to grow here." We take into account our own preferences and those of the clients at a homeless drop-in center where we send excess produce most of the year. We work to enrich the soil. The soil in turn enriches us. In good seasons, we approach harmony with the birds, bees, other insects, foraging critters, weeds, and cultivated plants with which we share this special plot of earth.

Chapter 7

What One Older American is Thinking and Needs to Say Out Loud

"Trump and my father (said) out loud what others are thinking but don't have the courage to say. They both were able to adopt the notion that fear and hate are the two greatest motivators of voters that feel alienated from government." —Peggy Wallace Kennedy, April, 2016

As the U.S. 2016 presidential campaign began heating up, I came across an interview with the daughter of former third party presidential candidate George Wallace of Alabama, most famously noted for having said in 1963, "Segregation now. Segregation tomorrow, and segregation forever." In late April of 2016, Peggy Wallace Kennedy suggested during a radio interview that the 1968 third party presidential candidacy of her late father had echoes in the 2016 campaign: "Trump and my father (said) out loud what others are thinking but don't have the courage to say. They both were able to adopt the notion that fear and hate are the two greatest motivators of voters that feel alienated from government."

As Mr. Trump's campaign, and then his presidency and ex-presidency have unfolded, many of his remarks have struck this older American as racist, misogynistic, xenophobic, jingoistic, reactionary, or all of the above. His tag line, "Make America Great Again," sometimes has led me to wonder when he thinks America was great, and for whom. Trump's signature slogan has become an acronym for a particular subset of extremist politics—"MAGA voters."

Mr. Trump and I were born within a year of each other. We are "leading edge boomers." We came into the world just after the end of World War II, when most countries in Europe and Asia were still reeling from the destruction of that conflict. American soldiers returning home were eager to leave the war behind them—their wives and girlfriends were equally eager to have their menfolk home. Together they created a "baby boom," with skyrocketing post-war birth rates that peaked in 1955.

Coming of age as a woman in the late 1960's and early 1970's, I found that a good many aspects of Trump's "great" America seemed less so to me:

Work: In 1970, about 80 percent of working age men were in the paid labor force, compared with just over 40% of women. Many professions were either completely barred to women, or had vastly differing entrance requirements for men and for women. Employment advertising was split by gender categories: "Help wanted, male" and "Help wanted, female." Women earned about 60 cents for every dollar earned by men for comparable work. By September, 2022, about 68% of working age men and 57% of working age women were in the paid labor force. Overall, women's earnings had reached roughly 83% of men's for comparable work, but with a greater lingering pay gap for mothers of all races and for women of color.

Roughly 30% of American jobs were in manufacturing in 1950. Since then, the proportion of manufacturing jobs has shown a near-continual decline, though the raw number of American manufacturing jobs peaked in 1979 at roughly 19.5 million workers. By 2022, only 13.8 million Americans (just over 8% of the overall paid labor force) worked in manufacturing. Some manufacturing job losses have been the result of outsourcing to lower wage countries. However, both in the U.S. and globally, many previous manufacturing jobs have been automated out of existence.

Immigration: Because of extremely restrictive U.S. immigration policies between 1917 and 1965, the proportion of foreign-born residents in the American population was at an all-time low at the 1970 census. Then, just 4.7% of Americans were foreign-born.

In 1965, the formerly nation-based quota system for U.S. immigration was overhauled, replaced by one favoring marketable skills and family reunification. Since then, both the numbers and proportion of foreign-born legal U.S. residents have increased, reaching a range of 12-15% of our current population. This influx is also partly due to increasing conflicts elsewhere in the world and to economic, social, and climate-based distress.

Nearly everyone admits that our current immigration system is overtaxed and flawed and needs another overhaul. However, national legislation to provide overall solutions to secure U.S. borders and to provide an orderly immigration pathway with minimal backlogs has repeatedly stalled in Congress. The failure to create an updated, coherent national immigration framework has resulted in a morass of conflicting rules and practices and helped to deepen crises at our borders.

Military: A military draft was most recently in force from 1948 through 1973. It affected young men aged 19 through 26. In 1969 and 1970, during the height of U.S. involvement in Vietnam, about half a million Americans served in that country each year, many of them draftees. The draft was ended in 1973. As the Vietnam War and later the Cold War wound down, active duty military personnel declined in numbers and as a proportion of the population. The post-World-War-II number of U.S. soldiers peaked in 1968 at about 3.5 million. Its current level is about 1.4 million, or less than half a percent of the total U.S. population. Between 160,000 and 180,000 troops have been stationed outside the U.S. in recent years.

Some other areas of concern in the late 1960's:
Race Relations
Environment
Women's Rights
Media
Political Culture

I share some of the frustrations that helped propel Mr. Trump into office in 2016. However, his more extreme rhetoric, along with the antics of his more extreme followers, have no place in a democracy. I believe we need to be more realistic and more complete, both about our recent American past and about our American prospects. Improvements in many Americans' lives since Mr. Trump and I were young have been substantial, but uneven, with periodic backsliding.

A truly great America depends on widespread participation and a basic level of trust. Further improvements are unlikely to take place in an atmosphere of fear and hatred. Much will continue to depend less on particular political candidates and

more on citizens' willingness to listen to each other and to say
out loud the pieces of the truth each of us knows.

Chapter 8

Whole Earth Generation(s)

"At the height of the civil-rights movement and the war in Vietnam, the "Whole Earth Catalog" offered a vision for a new social order—one that eschewed institutions in favor of individual empowerment, achieved through the acquisition of skills and tools."

—Anna Wiener, "The Complicated Legacy of Stewart Brand's 'Whole Earth Catalog'"

April 22 is now observed in many countries as "Earth Day." First celebrated in the United States in 1970, the event has gone global, drawing attention to environmental challenges and the need to cherish this planet, the only one that we know can support human life.

A little before the first Earth Day was celebrated, a low-cost, no-advertising catalog appeared: *The Whole Earth Catalog*. Editions were published about once a quarter during the years 1968-1972, and somewhat less regularly after that. Many editions carried on their cover an image of planet Earth as seen from space. The thrust of most entries was enabling individuals to become more self-sufficient, while also connecting with others along threads of common interest.

By the late 1960's, the excesses of unchecked industrialization and conspicuous consumption were starkly evident. The "boomer" generation I am part of, then coming of age in the U.S., had experienced less material deprivation than our parents' cohort. Instead, we'd been shaped by the political assassinations of the era, by proxy wars, by the rise of the civil rights and women's rights movements. We had a youthful desire for meaningful change. We thought we could make it happen, and soon! Teach-ins were a popular tool on a variety of issues. After viewing a massive 1969 oil spill off the coast of Santa Barbara, California, Wisconsin senator Gaylord Nelson hatched the idea for a national "teach-in" about the environment. It came to be called "Earth Day." Twenty million Americans participated, nearly ten percent of the total U.S. population at the time.

My new husband and I were looking for examples of more sustainable lifestyles. It may have been through a *Whole Earth Catalog*'s pages that we were introduced to the work and lives of Helen and Scott Nearing, a professional couple who during the 1930's left New York City at midlife and homesteaded successfully, first in Vermont and later in Maine. The Nearings lived off the land, grew their own food, built their own shelter, and wrote books and articles about their successes. We used their most famous work, *Living the Good Life: How to Live Simply and Sanely in a Troubled World*, as an inspiration for our transition from urban to simpler rural living. Unfortunately, when we tried to emulate the Nearings in the early 1970's, we soon learned that we lacked both the homesteading skills they exhibited and the resources or stamina to endure the periods of unemployment that were often part of rural life. We retreated to a mid-sized urban area where jobs were more plentiful and the worst excesses of conspicuous consumption were less in evidence. We have never given up on our dream of crafting a more sustainable lifestyle, though. We like to think we are making progress, if by fits and starts.

Culture and technology have changed a lot since 1970—the biggest threats to global health and stability can sometimes now be more diffuse and harder to tackle than the nation-state wars of preceding generations; civil rights and gender equality have made patchy, uneven, progress; telecommuting has made it more possible to reside in rural settings while still earning a living using mostly urban skills; the internet has out-stripped postal mail as a communications medium. However, some of the basics of human interactions have not changed all that much.

As a teen and then young adult, I was traumatized by the successive 1960's assassinations of JFK, MLK, and RFK. I mourned the loss of leaders who'd seemed to me to have some elements of the far-sighted vision America needed. For a while, I hoped for another external leader to appear to help move us along. Then I found a brief entry in the *Next Whole Earth Catalog*, put out in 1981, that provided a different perspective:

"If you notice that all the leaders who might make things better get shot you can:
  1) Assume their deaths were no coincidence and give up;
  2) Spend years proving their deaths were no coincidence and convincing others;
  3) Need leaders less."

Whenever our current crop of putative leaders leaves me unimpressed, I remind myself to need leaders less. Though some necessary global changes require large-scale interventions, many others can be carried out at an individual or small group level. "Saving the humans" (and many of the other species on which human life depends) requires varied efforts. Each of us can contribute.

The generation I'm part of is the first to have spent our entire adult lives with images of Earth in all its splendor and fragility as seen from outer space. The generations coming after ours were born with these images available. I hope they recognize both the beauty and the vulnerability of our home planet.

We could all use more principled, far-sighted leaders. Failing ready access to such rare humans, we need to remember that we each have within us both follower and leader. I hope that future "whole earth" generations will mature, find their paths, and need external leaders less.

Chapter 9

Stuck Between Levels

"We can't solve problems by using the same kind of thinking we used when we created them." —Albert Einstein

May can seem like an in-between month in many parts of the world—in the northern hemisphere, not quite full summer, yet past the first blush of spring. In the southern hemisphere, not yet full winter, yet getting colder and drearier as the days shorten. We can, in May, seem stuck.

Once, long ago, I got stuck in an elevator. It turned out to be a minor inconvenience, though a little scary at the time. I'd applied for a job in the new-to-me small town of Montpelier, Vermont. In order to finalize a preliminary job offer, I needed to complete some personnel paperwork and then be interviewed by two potential supervisors. The personnel office and these supervisors were in the same three-story building—personnel on the first floor, supervisors on the second. As I completed the final personnel forms, I noticed that it was almost time for my interviews. Rather than try to find the stairs, I took the elevator I'd passed in the main lobby on my way in. I was the only passenger.

The elevator got halfway to the second floor and stopped. I could see the upper floor through a ceiling gap above my head, but had no way to get out of the elevator to reach it. I pushed various control panel buttons, attempting to get the elevator unstuck, but nothing worked. I told myself not to panic—even if the elevator crashed to the basement, I'd probably survive with only minor injuries. If I didn't get the job, I could keep looking—I was well qualified and had gotten a good score on the relevant civil service exam. If this position didn't pan out, something else was bound to open up.

After a couple more rounds of futile button pushing, I finally hit the "send help" switch. In a few minutes, a repair technician appeared and solved the problem. Though I was a little late for the initial interview, the first supervisor who talked with me made light of my tardiness. He had recently gotten stuck in that same elevator. I got the job. Exiting the second interview, I found the stairway for any subsequent trips.

Lately it can seem hard to work our way out of the various global difficulties we humans have gotten ourselves into—a viral pandemic, nuclear and conventional arms races, air and water pollution, food insecurity, mass migrations, erratic weather, warming oceans, deforestation, income and wealth inequality. Our problems are sometimes exacerbated by distorted and distorting social media. We can often seem stuck.

Over the years, I've been exposed to many models that use the notion of levels to describe natural and/or human phenomena. One foundational model, the theory of evolution, describes how simple one-celled creatures have, over long timespans, spawned more and more complex life. On a human scale, models include Maslow's hierarchy of human needs, Piaget's stages of learning, Kubler-Ross's stages of grief. Some models include an explicit assumption that a shift to the "next level" is worthwhile. Often left implicit are the chaos and dis-comfort that can accompany a shift of levels, especially for us humans and especially when the systems are human-based.

When I was in school, teachers sometimes reminded us of a quote by scientist Albert Einstein: "We can't solve problems by using the same kind of thinking we used when we created them." Many of the difficulties we find ourselves in are, I believe, symptoms of ongoing level shifts. We're undergoing both a shift in our kind of thinking and a shift in social sys-tems we've created that no longer work very well, if they ever did. Perhaps the best we can do is avoid panic, diminish our need to be totally in control, learn when to hit the "send help" switch, and function as better repair technicians for the pieces of systems we know most thoroughly.

Chapter 10

Choosing Your Starfish

""It is a curious situation that the sea, from which life first arose, should now be threatened by the activities of one form of that life. But the sea, though changed in a sinister way, will continue to exist; the threat is rather to life itself."
—Rachel Carson, *The Sea Around Us*

Early in life, I became a fan of author and naturalist Rachel Carson when I received a copy of her 1951 book, *The Sea Around Us,* as a childhood Christmas present. Carson, born in May of 1907, is best known for a later book, *Silent Spring,* published in 1962. Extensively researched, that book cautions about the effects of overusing synthetic pesticides. Carson is credited by some as having helped launch the environmental movement of the 1960's and beyond. Although she died in 1964 of metastatic cancer, she leaves behind a rich legacy of environmental care. I often reread excerpts of her writings for perspective. Later, I came across another "sea" story also useful for perspective.

One of the years when I taught English in China, my students told me a story about an old man, a young boy, and a beach filled with stranded starfish. Many variants of the story exist. The one my students were most familiar with went something like this:

One morning after a storm, an older man went out for his customary walk along a gently curving stretch of beach. The weather had cleared. As he looked ahead, the man could see in the distance a small figure slowly walking in the same direction. Sometimes this person bent down, then threw something into the waves. As the older man got closer, he saw that the other person was a young boy, perhaps twelve years old. The stretch of beach nearest them was littered with stranded starfish. Once in a while, the boy leaned over, picked up a starfish, and tossed it back into the sea.

"You'll never succeed in making a difference for every living starfish," the old man cautioned. "There are too many of them, and they can't live very long on the beach."

"That's not the point," replied the boy as he tossed another starfish back into the waves. "I made a difference for that one."

I didn't remember having heard the story before. When I checked online for the story's origin, I found it had appeared in different form in 1969 as part of an essay titled "Star Thrower" by philosopher Loren Eiseley. The fable is both challenging and reassuring to me in these unsettled times. As someone with a tendency to obsess about any actual or potential "starfish" I may encounter, the story helps me regain balance. Of course I can never save all possible starfish. It's important, though, that I pay attention to the starfish who get stranded on "my" beach with problems that match my resources and the solution skills I've developed.

Who/what is your starfish?

Chapter 11

Joe McCarthy's Ghost, Slavery's Ghosts, Untangling Contexts

"Let us not assassinate this lad further, senator. You have done enough. Have you no sense of decency?"
—Joseph Welch, June 9, 1954

I began this piece on the morning of January 7, 2021, after 24 hours that tried American democracy in ways not seen for a while. Our electoral system survived, barely. Once an unruly mob was finally cleared from the U.S. Capitol, both houses of the U.S. Congress debated and then certified the electoral victory of Joseph R. Biden, Jr. to become the 46th President of the United States. However, challenges linger: a pandemic and its aftermath, continued misinformation and disinformation about the American electoral process, an abundance of social problems. The reputation of the U.S.A. as a beacon of democracy has been tarnished.

I was born into a United States of America emerging from World War II plus the dawn of the nuclear age. My childhood was spent in the shadow of possible thermonuclear war. Our family lived close to Washington D.C. A nuclear attack on the U.S. capital city would lead to our deaths—from the blast itself or more slowly from radiation poisoning. Nuclear danger from our main postwar rival, the communist Soviet Union (U.S.S.R.), was real but hard to gauge.

Postwar tensions had helped change the make-up of the U.S. Congress. During the early 1950's, a first-term Senator from Wisconsin made headlines about the alleged presence of "Communist infiltrators" in American government and media. Joseph R. McCarthy's initial list of possible infiltrators and spies grew ever longer, leading to the blacklisting of many left-leaning writers, artists and civil libertarians. In 1954, hearings about McCarthy's attempted meddling in the U.S. Army were broadcast on television between April and June, a TV first. The senator was shown, per multiple sources, as "bullying, reckless, and dishonest." Near the end of the hearings, at the end of his patience, Army Special Counsel Welch remarked: "Have you no sense of decency?" In retrospect, we realize that the distortions introduced by McCarthy made it more difficult to distinguish actual threats from malicious character assassination and misinformation. Later in 1954, McCarthy was censured by the U.S. Senate. Although he remained in office, his influence waned. He died of liver failure in 1957.

However, we still live with Joe McCarthy's ghost. One of McCarthy's chief advisors, Roy Cohn, went on to mentor real estate developer and 45th President of the United States, Donald J. Trump, a master at social media. Trump's posts and speeches surrounding the 2020 election helped incite what became on January 6, 2021 a full-blown riot. In the wake of that day's assault on the U.S. Capitol, some prominent social media outlets belatedly and temporarily deactivated Mr.

Trump's accounts. Nevertheless he continued, and continues, to spread false allegations about the election's outcome using whatever means he has available.

Our country's Declaration of Independence proclaims as self-evident that "all (men) are created equal, and that they are endowed by their Creator with certain unalienable Rights, that among these are Life, Liberty and the pursuit of Happiness." Those of us born in the U.S. are taught from an early age to revere this founding document. What we are not taught, or taught only much later, is that about a third of the signers of the Declaration, including coauthor Thomas Jefferson, were slaveholders.

We still live with slavery's ghosts. The inherent contradiction between professed equality and the myth of white supremacy poisons our civic life. During the summer of 2020, widespread multiracial demonstrations against police brutality and racial injustice highlighted flaws in our criminal justice system. Since the outbreak of covid-19 and related illnesses in the U.S., disparities in their impacts on communities of color have spotlighted lingering health and economic inequities. Our education system's attempts to adapt to remote learning further implicate the divides we've created and sustained in information access.

Many years ago, I was brought up in a mainline Protestant congregation, where I was taught the importance of loving our neighbors and ourselves. Other lessons were more mixed. A hymn we frequently sang back then started with a verse that can seem rife with the MAGA-style American exceptionalism and triumphalism that sometimes plague us now—sexist, militaristic, bombastic, shallow:

"Lead on, O King Eternal,
the day of march has come;

henceforth in fields of conquest,
thy tents shall be our home. ..."
I much preferred a different verse from the same hymn:
"Lead on, O King eternal,
till sin's fierce war shall cease,
and holiness shall whisper
the sweet amen of peace.
For not with swords loud clashing,
nor roll of stirring drums;
with deeds of love and mercy
the heavenly kingdom comes."

Searching for a partial antidote to 2021 post-insurrection anger and disgust, I delved into the origins of this hymn. The lyric was not intended militarily. It was composed by Ernest W. Shurtleff for his class's graduation ceremony from Andover Theological Seminary in 1887. It provided a rousing send-off for newly minted ministers. After graduation, Shurtleff served several American congregations before moving to Europe in 1905. From 1906 until the start of World War I, he was director of student activities at a Paris school. He then did war relief work in France until his death in Paris in 1917.

The inscription on Shurtleff's tombstone ends with this summation:

"The path of the just is
as the shining light."

May we follow this light through whatever darkness lies ahead. May we react to the January 6 travesties with outrage, yes, but also with deeds of love and mercy toward our neighbors and ourselves.

Chapter 12

On Being Temporarily Undocumented and Uncomfortable, More Permanently Advantaged

The Undocumented Resource Center (URC) at San Diego State University was created in 2020 through the efforts of Education Without Borders (EWB), students, staff, faculty, and alumni.
--sacd.sdsu.edu/undocumented-resource
(accessed 11/24/2022)

In mid-2021 I moved from central North Carolina to southern California. I was fortunate to have a choice in the timing and destination of my move. Still, moving always poses challenges. Now most members of my extended family were in a different time zone. Connections from my old location were broken. Our new household didn't have enough chairs. I didn't have a local doctor, dentist, or health care plan. I didn't have payment accounts for local utilities. I didn't know any of the local bakeries, take-out joints or restaurants. A good bit of the time, I felt lost. One of the most disorienting aspects of my "new life" was being relatively undocumented—no local driver's license, no local bank, no supermarket chain discount card, no voter ID, no links to local media. My challenges were minor, but I *so* wanted my uncertainty to end!

In my old location, I'd have labeled myself a white liberal if asked. I thought I'd worked through many issues surrounding whiteness in 21st century America. I'd listened to Rev. William Barber's impassioned, informative speeches about racial inequities. I'd participated in marches and protests, given money and time to progressive causes.

In my new location, few of the people around me were dark-skinned, but a lot looked somewhat different from me. Many spoke other languages instead of or in addition to English. I felt vaguely threatened.

Not long after the move, I got a packet of forwarded mail containing magazines with articles examining U.S. historical racism and unresolved racial and ethnic tensions. One article described the "race card project" started by journalist Michele Norris in 2010. She'd initially asked 200 people to send her their thoughts about race, distilled into just six words—a real challenge for somebody as wordy as I am! What popped into my head almost immediately was succinct, accurate, and embarrassing: "I thought I owned the place."

In school in the 1950's I'd been taught that European settlers had "conquered the wilderness," "shown pioneer spirit," "plowed the prairie," "expanded the frontier," "defeated the savage Indians," "fulfilled manifest destiny," etc., etc. Once I began to read and travel more widely, I learned some limits of this Eurocentric, English-centric viewpoint. In my new home, adding to my disorientation was discomfort at having to further reconfigure my former historical narrative. The version of U.S. history and growth I still partially carried around inside me was at best incomplete, at worst, deliberately falsified.

For thousands of years before the earliest European explorers came to North America, indigenous people lived in what is now the United States. Their claims to land ownership and stewardship were mostly ignored, the treaties they made with later settlers routinely violated. Many of their lives were cut short either by deliberate genocide or by their susceptibility to European-borne diseases.

Much of the hard manual labor to create the agricultural and industrial economies of our country was done, not by European settlers, but by either enslaved Africans or by poorly paid Chinese and other Asians. Currently, much agricultural and caregiving work is done by low-paid latinx immigrants.

Although the majority of my forebears in America didn't directly benefit from slavery or subsequent Jim Crow laws, they were "white" and therefore had access to financial support and government programs that were effectively, if not officially, biased in their favor. Explicit or implicit benefits from a system of arbitrary privilege can persist for generations, down to my own.

A few weeks after I arrived at our new home, I went to get a California driver's license at the local DMV. The people in line with me came in all shapes, colors, and sizes. They spoke with lots of different accents. Many DMV employees could speak two languages or even more. Might I have to own up to lingering biases, to adapt and participate in a more diverse culture here?

As I've gradually settled into our new-to-me location, it occurs to me that what I experienced on arrival was a new variant of the myth of white supremacy. This age-old scourge has for much of American history plagued our body politic. From time to time, an especially virulent strain has held sway, whether couched as "yellow peril" or "kung flu," as "happy darkies" or "welfare queens," as "wetbacks" or "job-stealing immigrants." Misrepresentations and discrimination against people who don't fit an evolving stereotype of "white America" diminish all of us. White supremacy is a malicious myth that needs to die.

When I'd previously lived in Richmond, Virginia for over a generation, one of its main avenues featured five monumental statues to Confederate military and political leaders, erected at the height of the Jim Crow era around the turn of the 20th century, partly to cow and diminish black citizens. Other less prominent monuments were scattered throughout the city. In December, 2022, the last remaining public Confederate monument in Richmond came down. Richmond's mayor was realistic about the city's progress toward inclusion and the distance remaining: "Over two years ago, Richmond was home to more confederate statues than any city in the United States. Collectively, we have closed that chapter. We now continue the work of being a more inclusive and welcoming place where all belong."

If we are ever to coalesce as a fully multi-ethnic society, we'll have to reject myths of dominance, white or otherwise. We'll have to call out and hold accountable purveyors and fomenters of political violence. If we've identified as "white," we'll have to more and more fully relinquish the myth of white supremacy. Instead, whoever we are, whatever our backgrounds, we'll need to more fully accept and embrace the humor, resilience, and graciousness that are part of everyone's human heritage.

Chapter 13

The Dangers of Hate Speech: Radio Mille Collines

Radio Télévision Libre des Mille Collines (RTLM) *was a Rwandan radio station which broadcast from July 8, 1993 to July 31, 1994. It played a significant role in inciting the Rwandan genocide that took place from April to July 1994, and has been described by some scholars as having been a de facto arm of the Hutu government.* —Wikipedia, accessed 11/24/2022

As someone born with a predisposition toward nervousness, I'm likely more put off than most by the name-calling and mud-slinging that too often inhabit media and political spaces in current-day America. From what I can tell, though, more and more of us are getting increasingly nervous about the state of our American body politic.

My natural predisposition was reinforced by exposure to some of the worst of human nature. In the mid-1980s, I spent two years as part of an international development project in the economically impoverished central African country of

Burundi. For most of its history, Burundi had been a sparsely populated, isolated mountainous kingdom with a preponderance of rural herders and farmers. Starting in the late 19th century, Burundi became briefly a German, then a Belgian colony, administered along with neighboring Rwanda. During their four-plus decades of rule, Belgian administrators often used "divide and conquer" tactics, exacerbating tensions between the area's two main ethnic groups. They pitted the Tutsis, most of whom owned and herded cattle, against the Hutus, who tended instead to farm multiple small plots owned communally by extended families in the Burundian and Rwandan hillsides, or "collines." Since its early 1960's independence, Burundi's trajectory had included political assassinations plus a massive ethnic conflict in the early 1970s that killed an estimated 300,000 Burundians.

When I first arrived, I spoke none of the local language, Kirundi. I had little notion of which of my coworkers and neighbors were Tutsi and which were Hutu. Physically similar, with the same language and skin tone, Tutsis and Hutus were sometimes characterized as "talls" and "shorts" in an exaggeration of one trait that distinguishes them at the extremes. During my stay, I gradually built up a very basic Kirundi vocabulary. Though fluency remained beyond my grasp, I understood enough so that when I attended a local soccer game partway through my assignment, I recognized the derogatory use of a word meaning "short." Some nearby spectators yelled it at the opposing team.

During the 1980s, Burundi and neighboring Rwanda were relatively calm, though ethnic tensions still simmered beneath the surface. In April, 1994, the then-presidents of both Burundi and Rwanda were killed when their plane was shot down as it returned to Kigali, Rwanda from an international trip. Both countries again descended into wholesale bloodletting, with the widely publicized Rwandan genocide of 1994 and a less-media-covered simmering civil war in Burundi. My prior experience in Burundi helped make me a horrified, if long-distance witness to this resurgence of hate-induced wholesale slaughter. Part of the build-up to the Rwandan genocide consisted of incitements by a privately owned radio station, Radio Mille Collines (Radio of a Thousand Hillsides), against ethnic Tutsis and moderates of all groups. According to a summary by the Montreal Institute for Genocide and Human Rights Studies:

"From October 1993 to late 1994, Radio-Television-des-Mille-Collines (RTLM) was used by Hutu leaders to advance an extremist Hutu message and anti-Tutsi disinformation, spreading fear of a Tutsi genocide against Hutu, identifying specific Tutsi targets or areas where they could be found, and encouraging the progress of the genocide. In April 1994, Radio Rwanda (the official government station) began to advance a similar message, speaking for the national authorities, issuing directives on how and where to kill Tutsis, and congratulating those who had already taken part."

After the genocide and a change of government in Rwanda, international criminal proceedings brought to trial some of the political leaders of genocide-era Rwanda, along with some of the media leaders who had helped foment hatred with their increasingly strident broadcasts. Not all ringleaders could be located and brought to justice, but 92 high-ranking defendants were indicted for their roles in a 100-day rampage that killed an estimated 800,000 Rwandans.

I sometimes fear for my own country and for our planet. Derogatory speech is again on the rise globally, whether from politicians, media pundits, or just disgruntled citizens and residents. Americans belonging to groups who have in the past been targets of repression and/or genocide—native Americans, African-Americans, Jews, immigrants, LGBTQ persons, among others—feel the impact most deeply, but it affects us all. As one European Jewish leader put it, "While hate speech and incitement is far too often dismissed as bigoted ranting or merely painful words, it can also serve as an important warning sign for much more severe consequences. Almost every genocide, ethnic cleansing or inter-ethnic conflict in modern history was preceded by violent words. We witnessed inflammatory public speech rise steadily before outbreaks of mass violence, whether in Nazi Germany, Rwanda or in the former Yugoslavia."

Free speech is a fundamental right of democratic governance. It is included as part of the first amendment to the U.S. Constitution. Of course we need to be able to express varying views, but we need to exercise our free speech right thoughtfully and civilly, rather than by using name-calling, blaming, or personal attacks. Free speech is not the same as hate speech or incitement—please let us learn and teach the difference.

Chapter 14

The Rest of
the Story

Don't let noisy news distress you. Don't let the headline writers rain on your parade. My goodness, there's resiliency in this country. —Paul Harvey (undated video clip)

The late 1960's were a turbulent time, not unlike the period we're living through now. Starting in 1965, I attended a small liberal arts college in a mid-sized Virginia city. Through my studies and socializing, I was exposed to professors and fellow students from a variety of backgrounds, with a variety of opinions. Some were quite different from the prevailing views in the small Maryland town where I'd spent my first 18 years. Off campus, though, prevailing sentiments were every bit as conservative as those I'd grown up with.

Sometimes I'd listen to a local radio station to catch a weather report for the upcoming weekend. The weather forecast was part of a longer news program, so I often wound up exposed to all or part of a nationally syndicated broadcast by radio announcer Paul Harvey. I remember only a little specific content from Paul Harvey's broadcasts, but I recall a general tone. His style has been characterized as valuing "rugged individualism, love of God and country, and the fundamental decency of ordinary people."

Through my newly expanded collegiate lens, it seemed to me that Harvey was leaving out huge parts of the news that didn't coincide with his perspective. I was seeing firsthand instances of housing and employment discrimination, experiencing the escalation of the Vietnam war, noting the routine harassment of minorities and women. I was learning of historic lynchings. None of this seemed fundamentally decent. I began to question some of Harvey's premises. With collegiate self-righteousness, I thought I'd grown beyond Harvey's views.

One especially celebrated Paul Harvey segment was called "The Rest of the Story," typically a relatively unknown part of the life story of a famous person. One of the most widely broadcast and rebroadcast was about a high school dropout, "Al." In his early 20's, Al applied for an entry level job at the Swiss patent office. He nearly didn't get it. Not until the end of the segment were we told that, despite early life reverses, "Al" eventually went on to become world-famous as theoretical physicist Albert Einstein.

These days I have a schizoid relationship with media. I need to stay informed, but too often a media broadcast or internet post leaves me inflamed instead. It is difficult to follow any news source for long without buying into some of its inherent biases. Images of a violent mob storming the U.S. Capitol on January 6, 2021 are hard to ignore. Is there a rest of the story? Temporarily putting aside the role of Mr. Trump, what were the varying motivations that led some to become violent, others to remain bystanders, while most of America's population stayed away? Is there anything to be learned from the life histories of those who demonstrated, those who desecrated, those who tried to defuse tensions, those who tried to maintain order, and/or those who attempted to report live as events unfolded?

Few of the reports I've heard yet provide much insight. Too often I get competing narratives that emphasize conflicting aspects of reality. About the only commonality seems to be that all of us are tense.

We are never likely to know the whole story. Imperfect, incomplete knowledge is part of the human condition. However, if we listen more, if we do the messy work of decoupling legitimate grievances from scapegoating and vengeance, if we insist on both accountability and mercy, we may learn more of the rest of the story.

Chapter 15

Fear Sells, Until...

Over time, we've come to see nuclear weapons as Hersey (author of Hiroshima, *first published in 1946) saw them, as the ultimate expression of material and spiritual evil of total war. The bomb has come to represent the ability of our civilization to destroy itself, and our nagging fear that our political and social institutions are inadequate to save us from the abyss.*
—Jeffrey Lewis, August 6, 2015 in *Foreign Policy*

August 6 is observed in some countries as Hiroshima Day. It commemorates the first military use of nuclear weapons, when an atomic bomb dropped from an American plane detonated above the Japanese city of Hiroshima. Casualty figures have been difficult to confirm. It's estimated that somewhere between 110,000 and 210,000 people died as a result of the blast. The anniversary underscores the increasing capacity of us humans to annihilate ourselves. It can reinforce a fear that our species has technologically outdistanced our capacity to use our technology wisely. This fear, always a subconscious part of my life, is one I've struggled to come to terms with. I study and work and pray to find ways to overcome it. Being an engaged citizen is one way I cope.

On a spring weekend in 2016, I went with a small group of peaceful protesters from Raleigh, North Carolina to Washington, D.C. to encourage more transparency in campaign financing, along with less influence from huge, often difficult-to-trace donors. I also wanted to network with younger activists and to support wider participation in our democracy. I attended workshops, met with old friends, made new ones.

Later that same year, I attended a " Decision 2016" rally in Raleigh, N. C., headlined by Franklin Graham, son and heir to crusading evangelist Billy Graham.

The constituencies at the two events had little overlap, but themes of fear and "othering" were endemic at both—at the first, fear of big corporations and wealthy individuals coopting our democracy; at the second, fear of losing our religious underpinnings as a society. Sometime during that year, I bought a small lapel button: "Fear sells, until you stop buying it."

These days, groups and media outlets from all across the political spectrum want to sell me fear. Rarely a day goes by when I'm not assaulted by various postal, email, televised, or social media entries explaining why "others" are destroying the world as we know it, why everything will be lost unless I subscribe to some variation of their views. It can get so intense that I sometimes zone out temporarily. The combination of media frenzy and a lingering pandemic caused by a pathogenic virus can leave many of us feeling isolated and in dread of what's "out there."

When the cacophony of disparate media voices gets too loud, I switch off even those opinions I mainly agree with. I silence the television, ignore the internet, power down my cell phone. Often, I go outdoors. In addition to lessening the likely danger from viruses, spending time out in nature helps me to experience once more my minor role but valued place in the grand scheme of things. Away from traffic and mechanical noise, I can reconsider. I can remember to honor the humanity of those with whom I disagree. I can ponder what my own fears are and how I can reduce them. I need to take such intervals to drop into the deeper reaches of my nature, to reconnect with the underlying wholeness of the cosmos.

The relative isolation of pandemic life has paradoxically given me more chances to experience this deeper connection. I've had a hiatus in which to face some fears, to strengthen my resistance. As I gradually free myself from fear and isolation, I can participate more fully and effectively in joint actions to make long-needed changes to the ways we humans have organized ourselves. I can help strengthen the political and social institutions that pull us back from the abyss.

Of course fear still sells to me sometimes, but its market share is dwindling.

Chapter 16

What Difference Can a Letter Make?

"The right of citizens of the United States to vote shall not be denied or abridged by the United States or by any State on account of sex."
—19th Amendment to the U.S. Constitution

I'm a fan of the United States Postal Service. What is now the USPS was first established in 1792 under President George Washington. It has undergone several reorganizations since. The service has been especially valuable to me during periods when I've resided outside the United States. Then, it provided the surest way for me to interact with family and friends back home. Internet access might be absent or spotty, cell phone towers and/or phone lines might go down in earthquakes or other natural disasters, but the mail somehow nearly always got through.

On August 26, many in the U.S. celebrate Women's Equality Day, marking the anniversary of the 19th Amendment to the U.S. constitution for women's suffrage: "The right of citizens of the United States to vote shall not be denied or abridged by the United States or by any State on account of sex." Some women activists know the story of the letter that made a difference in the suffrage fight—a six-page handwritten missive from a widowed mother to her son, Harry T. Burn, a 24-year-old Republican lawmaker from McMinn County, Tennessee.

After hearing a scathing denunciation of the amendment by one of her son's legislative mentors in the Tennessee General Assembly, Febb Burn was moved to include a gentle rebuttal in her letter, nestled among descriptions of doings on the family farm. She closed with a suggestion, "Don't forget to be a good boy and help Mrs. Catt...(a longtime suffragist)." When Burn broke a previous tie in the Tennessee legislature to support suffrage, others at first thought he'd made a mistake. He had not. He'd opted for conscience and the advice of his mother over political expedience in his heavily conservative district.

My family has a different letter that made a difference. It was written by an Army corporal serving in Germany during the waning days of World War II. My uncle, John Voris, loved learning. He described in his letter that he'd sent a big batch of books home, and hoped for a new shipment soon. "About the books, ... I try to keep one or two about me all the time. You see that four years in the army represents a big hole in your life. I try to keep studying and reading so that I can salvage some of these years, in part at least."

Much of the November, 1944 letter describes his prior campaigns and the bronze star he'd just been awarded. What made and makes the letter special is that it was received by his family at about the same time as the telegram informing them that he had been killed in action. While the letter couldn't bring John back, it helped assuage their grief. His younger sister, a printer, had the letter typeset and distributed. It has been passed down from generation to generation. Along with a few pictures, it's a reminder of an idealistic young soldier who didn't live to see the next peacetime.

The Febb Burn letter is now displayed in a museum. Most family mementoes have a less illustrious place, but they are still special. Our emails, tweets and instagram posts are never likely to replace a thoughtful, newsy letter. So take the time to write a postal letter to someone you care about. Letters *can* make a difference.

Chapter 17

Still Subtle and Various and Human

"(September 2, 1939) *The Germans are steaming ahead into Poland; all negotiations are off. Even the news becomes not diplomatic but military, not subtle and various and human but clear and cold and metallic.*"
--Anne Morrow Lindbergh, *War Without and Within*

Recent election cycles in the U.S. have provided quite a roller coaster ride. Now that another campaign cycle is gearing up, I'm trying to direct my attention away from tendencies toward increasingly negative and personality-centered political campaigns.

What gives me some hope for positive change are recent conversations I've been having with family, friends and acquaintances of various political persuasions. At least some of these interactions have been getting deeper without getting rancorous. My sample size is small. However, among those with whom I've gingerly broached the subject of American politics, what stands out to me are the variations in both motivations and reactions. I've not found consensus. Nevertheless, the opinions I've heard are more nuanced than much of what I'm exposed to in most media.

I also draw some encouragement from polling that seems to show a diverse electorate attempting to sift through multiple issues and challenges. A 2022 "American values" poll cited by financial magazine *Forbes* indicated that about 40 percent of Americans would favor a new, more centrist political party instead of the two major parties we currently have. An increasing proportion of American voters are registering as independents (or, in California, with "no party preference"). Per political tracking website Ballotpedia, in October, 2022, there were nine U.S. states where non-affiliated voters were a larger proportion of the electorate than either Democrats or Republicans (Alaska, Arkansas, Colorado, Connecticut, Massachusetts, New Hampshire, North Carolina, Oregon, and Rhode Island).

Though I'm now part of an older, supposedly wiser generation, I find myself wishing that my parents' "greatest generation" were still around in large enough numbers to inject more wisdom into our media mix. I take some solace from one of the lesser-known volumes authored by Anne Morrow Lindbergh, best known as the writer of the 1950's classic *Gift from the Sea.* Anne's early life was sheltered and privileged—one of four children of a successful businessman-turned-ambassador. In 1929, she married famed aviator Charles Lindbergh. She came to maturity as global politics darkened during the 1930's. After the kidnapping and murder of their eldest child in New Jersey in 1932, she and her husband for several years sought refuge and privacy in England. By 1939, Anne was back in the U.S., tending a growing household while publicly supporting her husband's strong isolationist opinions. Anne viewed events in Europe with increasing alarm. Parts of her personal journals from the period 1939-1945 were published much later, in

1980, as *War Without and Within*. I found the lead-in to her entry for September 2, 1939 especially compelling:

"The Germans are steaming ahead into Poland; all negotiations are off. Even the news becomes not diplomatic but military, not subtle and various and human but clear and cold and metallic."

We will elect our next crop of public officials while facing many possible problems and challenges, including a war in Europe that threatens to escalate into another global conflict, plus a lingering global pandemic and a longer-term threat from accelerating climate change. Each of us has various experiences, opinions, and expertise with which to cope with these challenges.

Some choices will seem stark; others may be difficult. Still, we have the capacity to recall that we as Americans, and as citizens of the world, can be subtle and various and human, if only we choose to do so.

Chapter 18

Seven Harmful/ Helpful Political Habits

"Celebrated every September, National Voter Registration Day involves volunteers and organizations from all over the country hitting the streets in a single day of coordinated field, technology and media efforts. National Voter Registration Day seeks to create broad awareness of voter registration opportunities to reach tens of thousands of voters who may not register otherwise." —nationalvoterregistrationday.org/about (accessed 11/18/2022)

Citizens in a democracy are constituents in multiple levels of government, however we choose to view ourselves. Voting is one cornerstone of democratic government. Protecting the right to vote and participating in honest and fair elections are responsibilities we all share. Over the years, though, I developed a variety of bad political habits. Sometimes I even dropped out of participating in an election altogether. However, I'm doing my best to reform some of my bad habits, to become and to stay engaged and informed, to participate fully. Here's my list of bad habits, with some hints for countermeasures:

1) Local politics does not matter.

I can too easily focus on the "big" political races, glossing over the reality that the government level that impacts me most directly is local: local budgets; local public safety; local tax rules and rates; school funding; zoning; the placement and maintenance of roads, parks, and greenways; economic development plans and procedures; environmental safeguards and incentives; local voting rules; the placement of voting sites. In addition to "big" races, I also need to pay attention locally.

2) Politics is dirty. Most politicians are crooks. I don't trust the system.

Our national, state and local political scandals can seem endless. Journalists make reputations by ferreting out officials' misdeeds. Politicians whose positive program proposals are lacking often instead stress the negative aspects of their opponents and/or the opposing political party. "Dark money" (large, difficult to trace contributions) can distort our elections. I often hear unsubstantiated claims of widespread voter fraud. It can be tempting either to walk away from politics or to act out my frustrations with the system violently.

Active citizenship demands both enthusiasm and restraint. I can play a useful part through small monetary donations, thoughtful social media posts, in-kind donations, and/or labor in support of candidates and causes of my choice. I can vary the sources of my "partial" news (almost never impartial or complete) to try to understand multiple perspectives. Most important of all, even when possibilities seem less than ideal, *I can vote*. The right to vote can be eroded through outright coercion, but also through disuse.

3) Government can solve all our problems.

I can let my expectations of government get overblown. Sometimes I fantasize that my elected officials can just snap their fingers and quickly reduce negative impacts of pandemics, globalization, or automation; can minimize unemployment while controlling inflation; can eliminate child poverty; can mitigate climate change; can usher in world peace. In more realistic moments, I acknowledge that expecting governments to do too much or too quickly can be self-defeating. I can nudge my elected officials in what I consider to be worthwhile directions. I can get and stay informed. I can make a small difference; many small differences *do* add up.

4) Government *is* the problem.

Sometimes I've lost my temper in conversations with "faceless bureaucrats" over regulations I thought were obsolete, needlessly harsh, or downright stupid. I can find parts of government maddeningly unresponsive, from the local to the federal level.

It's far easier for me to remember government actions that inconvenience me or limit my perceived choices than to remember valuable government services, from filling potholes on damaged roads to providing fire, police, and military protection, to dispensing veterans' benefits, to underwriting healthcare subsidies for the elderly and the poor. Governing is complex. Getting it "right" takes both hard effort and principled compromise.

5) If we just elect the right candidates, all will go well.

Voting for a successful candidate is no guarantee that the policies he/she advocates will get implemented. Our political system was designed to have checks and balances. Since the U.S. first became a nation, our national population has increased nearly a hundred fold. Officials at many levels represent increasingly diverse populations—in their districts, their state, or our nation as a whole. However much they want to serve their constituents and our nation well, the job is extremely difficult. Personal attacks only make a hard job harder.

If I want the elected officials who represent me to reflect my views, voting is an important first step, but not the only one. I also need to remind successful candidates of my views on issues—coherently, respectfully, and repeatedly.

6) "Watershed" elections are crucial; some losses are irreversible.

Of course it matters which political party controls government appointments and legislative committee assignments. Of course congressional and presidential elections matter. However, as I've lived through more and more election cycles, I've come to believe that hyperbole about potential shifts in policy as a result of a single election can be counterproductive. Many substantive changes take decades or even generations. Conversations and disagreements in our society about the rights, responsibilities, and roles of minorities and women have existed since our beginnings as a nation. They continue to this day.

I'm skeptical of overblown claims, both of potential disaster from a single election, and of single-election long-term gains. However, it *is* important to vote in *every* election, not just the high profile ones. It *is* important to stay engaged and informed, regardless of who holds the presumed power at any given time.

7) Politics is serious business, so we all need to engage in it with utmost seriousness.

One casualty of the recent enhanced nastiness in politics is the decline of the "smiling candidate." Too often, our media feeds and social networks send us scowling images of "those others," whoever various media algorithms have decided they might be. We need to remember that successful politicians of many different persuasions, from Ronald Reagan to Nelson Mandela, learned to take themselves lightly while taking their causes seriously. Even in these polarized times, it *is* possible to be well-reasoned, polite, even humorous. A wise mentor once told me, "A smile is the shortest distance between two points of view."

Presidential elections occur at four year intervals. Congressional elections occur every two years, with many jurisdictions holding local elections in the odd-numbered "off" years. Chances are there's another election cycle approaching where you live. Please continue to do the vital work of reforming whatever your bad political habits happen to be. Above all, *please* make it a habit to keep your voter registration current, and *please* vote—in every election!

Chapter 19

On to Kyiv, and Then What?

"Ukrainian forces battled Russian forces on three sides on Thursday after Moscow unleashed the biggest attack on a European state since World War Two, prompting tens of thousands of people to flee their homes."
—Reuters, February 24, 2022

Like many globally in our media-saturated environment, I'm distressed about the invasion of Ukraine by its larger neighbor Russia. For weeks prior to the invasion, we saw reports of a buildup of Russian troops and military equipment along the borders with Ukraine. As I write this, nearly a year after the initial invasion, winter has set in. Ukrainian soldiers have succeeded in pushing back Russian troops in some areas, amid fierce fighting and conflicting claims. Damage to Ukrainian infrastructure is extensive. Many lives have been lost—soldiers on both sides, plus civilians, most of them Ukrainian. Millions have been displaced, either internally or across borders. Russia's aims are not totally clear. Most American pundits tell us that Russia's authoritarian ruler, Vladimir Putin, wants to topple the existing Ukrainian government and install a regime more to his liking. Some more sympathetic toward Putin say that the West is partially responsible for the conflict, having helped stoke fears of an expanded NATO at Russia's very doorstep. Whatever the rationale, the results have been disastrous.

Over the centuries, nation-states have come and gone, along with empires and dynasties. Invasion and conquest are scenarios that have played out countless times throughout history whenever a superior military power desired to dominate its neighbor(s). The United States of America has not always been immune to utilizing conquest, despite our protestations of "spreading democracy," and so on. The impulse to conquest seems to be part of our human heritage, from the earliest cave dweller with a bigger club, through the desolation wrought by 1940's era blitzkrieg, concentration camps, kamikaze attacks, fire bombings and atomic bombs. During the 1990's, a massive genocide in Rwanda was conducted mostly with machetes. We've had multitudes of wars using "more conventional" weaponry both before and since.

Problems can arise in the aftermath of a military conquest, as we've seen recently and tragically in contemporary Afghanistan. Conquering and governing are two substantially different domains. If a new regime gets installed, who repairs the infrastructure that's been damaged or destroyed during the conquest? Who provides the basic necessities—food, clothing, shelter—to a cowed, needy, and probably sullen civilian population? Who attempts to reestablish borders and to stem the outflow of brain and talent of those eager and able to leave? Who works to reduce the likelihood that resentments will fester and eventually result in further armed conflicts when the balance of military power shifts?

I've never traveled in Ukraine. Prior to the current war, my main point of reference was the 1986 nuclear meltdown at Chernobyl, a now-decommissioned power plant near the Ukrainian/Russian border, about 70 miles from Kyiv. Much earlier, I was taught courses in Russian language and culture by a college professor who'd escaped from Ukraine during the final days of World War II. When "Dr. K." taught us, the Union of Soviet Socialist Republics, which then included Ukraine, was near its height. The Cold War was raging. The availability of non-official information about conditions in any socialist republic was severely limited. As our language facility in Russian improved, Dr. K. showed us articles from the Soviet press that glorified the Soviet state without mentioning any possible problems.

Because of the tightly controlled Soviet media environment, many of us outside the U.S.S.R. (and some inside the decaying giant) were largely unaware of internal problems until an undeniable plume of Chernobyl-released radioactivity crossed into the rest of Europe. We were likewise ill prepared for the dissolution of the Soviet empire several years later. In some sense, all of us, whatever our views on Ukraine, are still trying to come to terms with the aftermath.

If we are to survive as a species, it seems to me that we humans need to rein in our thirst for conquest, and rather to cultivate our countervailing impulse to nurture. The members of the military I know best and most admire are much more eager to assist after natural or man-made disasters than they are eager for combat and conquest. Dealing with the disaster of a global viral pandemic, recent horrific earthquakes in Turkey and Syria, plus a slower-moving planet-wide disaster of climate change, can use all our ingenuity and empathy. These disasters call out for the greatest exercise of our nurturing sides that we can muster.

If Kyiv falls, then what?

Chapter 20

On Being Granted Three Witches

"I've heard it said that people come into our lives for a reason..."
—Witch Glinda, "For Good," from the musical *Wicked*

Many years around Hallowe'en, we used to get inundated with images of "wicked witches." Lately, though, our understanding of witches has undergone something of a change, abetted by a modern Wiccan movement. Performances such as "Wicked," a musical retelling of the Wizard of Oz story from the point of view of two witches, have also reminded us of the "good witch." Since I moved to southern California a couple of Hallowe'ens ago, it's been my good fortune to become acquainted with three very good witches, three benign elders. They've helped me begin to feel at home in this new-to-me locale where I hope also to become a beneficial elder.

The first good witch I encountered was Anne, a spritely octogenarian with a halo of blue-white curls. When I first met her, Anne was presiding over a large table of other elders at a summer neighborhood gathering of a "village," a mutual help group for over-55's who want to continue to live in their own homes for as long as possible, rather than moving to assisted living facilities. Anne was one of the original members of our local group a dozen years ago. Listening to some of Anne's stories, I learned that she had spent time in China, a favorite travel destination of mine earlier in life. I asked if I might meet with her one-on-one to trade stories, to learn more about her China experiences. She graciously acceded. Anne's China stay had occurred mostly before I was born. She was a school girl in Shanghai and then in Chongqing from 1946 to 1948 while her naval officer father was an advisor to the Chinese military.

Anne's life experiences are quite different from mine—a Navy daughter, then a Navy wife to a commander who served during Vietnam, a conflict I had protested as a young woman. Anne raised a large family while moving from military post to post and adhering to her Roman Catholic faith. Her opinions on reproductive freedom are likely different from mine. However, she has never tried to proselytize or to foist her views on me. She has expressed that aspect of her faith mostly through work with charities and social service agencies in support of adoptive parents, support often badly needed.

My next good witch encounter was with Carolyn. As I oriented myself to our new environment by walking around, I was pleased that our "planned community" of about 700 houses had pleasant walkways and little traffic. A couple of small strip shopping centers bracketed the complex. A nearby public recreation area had both indoor and outdoor athletic facilities. Near the top of the closest hill was a cluster of churches. One morning as I explored the grounds of the local Lutheran church, I noticed a fenced garden behind the main building, with numbered raised plots and a small sign identifying it as a "nature friendly garden." No one was around. I opened the garden gate and walked through the area. At one end were a small red shed and a small greenhouse. A couple of wrought iron lawn chairs were pulled up in front of the shed. The place looked well tended. I gradually made it a regular part of my walking routine. Several walks later, I came across Carolyn, tending some of the many plots she cares for. She'd opened the padlocked shed and was ferrying garden tools and containers back and forth as needed. She finished what she was doing, then took a break to chat.

"This garden has been my sanity refuge during covid," she told me. "Outdoors, so less virus-prone, and still able to provide a service to the community." She explained that most of "her" beds contained vegetables planted for use at T.A.C.O. (Third Avenue Charitable Organization), a downtown San Diego drop-in center for the area's homeless and lower income residents. On Thursdays, Carolyn ferried fresh produce from her T.A.C.O. beds to the center to be included in the following day's lunch. She'd been doing this since well before the pandemic. Given the disproportionate impact of the pandemic on those already struggling, she felt it was more needed during covid than ever.

"It's amazing what the cooks can do with whatever I bring," she said. "Sometimes we have mostly zucchini, other times it's tomatoes, or carrots, or broccoli, or cabbage. Some of the other gardeners contribute their extra veggies as well." Carolyn isn't shy about her age—mid-80's. She complains that she's slowing down, but she can still heft a flat of squash or spade a garden plot with more energy than most of us, whatever our ages.

Ellen introduced herself to me by phone before I met her in person. She's the doyenne of volunteers at our local public library branch. A restriction of pandemic lockdowns that hit me hard was the closure of area libraries. As soon as infection numbers waned enough so that libraries reopened, I visited our nearest branch. I checked out as many books as I could carry and signed up as a "Friend of the Tierrasanta Library." Several months later, Ellen phoned to ask if I might be available to help cashier for a two-hour shift at the used book sale she and others arranged in the library's conference room during the first weekend of every month.

"Sure," I said. "Do I need to bring anything?"

"Just yourself. You'll be working with an experienced volunteer who can show you what to do." Ellen, too, complains that she is slowing down. Well into her 80's, she's had one hip replaced and is due to get the second one done this year. At the end of a day's work, she has a noticeable limp. She doesn't let it deter her much.

For over thirty years, it turns out, Ellen has been raising money for the library and spreading the love of books throughout the community. She has over time refined a system that supplies extra children's books at no charge to a nearby military housing complex.

Not long after arriving in California, I passed the midway point between 70 and 80. I'm slowing down some. Aging has brought different challenges. One of the hardest for me is balancing self care with care for the wider community. Initially constrained by covid and by my general lack of knowledge of how this part of the country works, I've been inspired by the lives of my three good witches. Anne, Carolyn, and Ellen are not native Californians, either. They've all passed the 80 year milestone. Their adaptability and continuing active participation shine forth. Somewhere near here are adoptive families with better coping skills thanks to Anne; someday a needy person is getting a more nutritious lunch thanks to Carolyn; in some child's room someone is reading thanks to Ellen.

My skills are not exactly the same as theirs. Still, I can write about them, mimic them as much as I can, encourage others to follow their examples. You likely know some good witches, too.

Chapter 21

Practicing Gestational Political (November 9, 2016)

Now that we in the United States of America have elected a prime verbal ejaculator to be our putative leader, it will not do for women to turn our hurt and anger inward. It will not be enough merely to cry out in rage and disgust. What we must do instead is to take a short respite, then to return with renewed dedication to building bridges across the chasms of gender, race, class, urban/rural, national origin and affection that this retrograde campaign has made more evident. We must nurture ourselves, along with the next generations of humans and of other creatures on this lovely planet.

Chapter 22

Selective Memory and Finishing the Work We Are In

"Shortly after noon on November 22, 1963, President John F. Kennedy was assassinated as he rode in a motorcade through Dealey Plaza in downtown Dallas, Texas." —JFK Memorial Library

Like most folks, I have a selective memory. On Friday, November 22, 1963, I was a Maryland high school student. I remember hearing the beginning of an announcement over the school's public address system that day at an unusual time for announcements. As the announcement continued, I remember coming down the stairwell between two floors of our building, along with many other students changing classes.

I don't remember if the announcement I heard while going downstairs was the first—that President Kennedy had been shot—or the second—that he had shortly afterward been pronounced dead at a Dallas hospital. I don't remember whether school that day was dismissed early or whether school was canceled the following Monday for his funeral. I don't remember much about that year's Thanksgiving the following Thursday.

The previous year, there had been a tense standoff between the nuclear-armed U.S.A. under Kennedy's leadership, and the nuclear-armed U.S.S.R. under Nikita Khrushchev. At issue were nuclear missiles recently installed by the U.S.S.R. on the island of Cuba, just 90 nautical miles from Florida's Key West. I remember that my dad built a nuclear fallout shelter in our front yard at about that time, but I don't remember whether it was before or after Kennedy was shot.

Parts of our education when I was a student involved memorizing famous poems and speeches. I can recite most of a short Abraham Lincoln speech from a century earlier, first spoken in November, 1863 at a dedication ceremony for a military cemetery at the site of one of the U.S. Civil War's deadliest battles:

"Four score and seven years ago our fathers brought forth on this continent, a new nation, conceived in Liberty, and dedicated to the proposition that all men are created equal. Now we are ...testing whether that nation, or any nation so conceived and dedicated, can long endure.... It is ... for us to be here dedicated to the great task remaining before us ... that we here highly resolve that these dead shall not have died in vain — that this nation, under God, shall have a new birth of freedom — and that government of the people, by the people, for the people, shall not perish from the earth."

In the tragic days after Lincoln's assassination in April, 1865, his Gettysburg speech was nearly forgotten. Later, the contents of the speech took on more importance. When the current Lincoln Memorial was dedicated in Washington, D.C. in 1922, the Gettysburg Address was inscribed on one of the monument's inside walls. When as a teen I visited the monument,

I remember gazing up at Lincoln's statue, puzzling at what seemed to me a mixture of sadness and resolve on the former President's face. I remember cherry blossoms falling into the tidal pools in the parkland surrounding the monument.

We are now experiencing more tests of the viability of democratic institutions, in the U.S. and elsewhere. Although the linkage is not totally clear, we may also be testing the limits of continuing human viability on this planet. Scientists tell us that the world's nations and their citizens have only a decade or so to drastically curb our net output of climate-warming gasses if we are to maintain a planet capable of supporting human life as we know it.

On another wall of the Lincoln Memorial is his second inaugural, delivered in 1865 just over a month before his assassination:

"With malice toward none, with charity for all, with firmness in the right as God gives us to see the right, let us strive on to finish the work we are in, to bind up the nation's wounds, to care for him who shall have borne the battle... to do all which may achieve and cherish a just and lasting peace among ourselves and with all nations."

In November, 2022, leaders and thinkers from around the world again gathered to attempt to hammer out agreements and strategies to avoid overheating the planet that supports all human life. Perhaps each of us can summon a memory of the splendor of our existing earth to help us strengthen democratic institutions while we finish this work we are in.

Chapter 23

Learned Helpfulness

"Optimists recover from their momentary helplessness imme-diately. Very soon after failing, they pick themselves up, shrug, and start trying again."
　　　　　—Martin Seligman, from *Learned Optimism*

Most of our recent news is bad: warfare in Ukraine, mass shootings in the U.S., wildfires, floods, tornados, hurricanes, blizzards, earthquakes. The list seems endless. It helps me to remember that most news has always been bad. We tend to take for granted the generosity, kindness, humor, and love that people bestow on each other much of the time. Pleasant weather is considered unremarkable. We rarely get headlines or breaking news about the nice people or the nice weather. It's the bad examples, the exceptions, that get the bulk of the publicity. Through our increasingly interconnected global communications, we can more readily and extensively broad-cast the negative aspects of reality. They are not the whole picture.

Recently, an overload of news about wars and mass shoot-ings and refugees and climate crises and teen anxiety and so on tempted me to lapse into "learned helplessness." This is a psychological condition often linked with depression. Problems can seem just too overwhelming to deal with.

Instead, I made a conscious attempt to find some good news. I started with a basic internet search on altruism, broadly defined as actions taken on behalf of others that provide little or no benefit to the altruist. I watched several "Kindness 101" segments created by CBS reporter Steve Hartman in 2020, early in the covid pandemic, when he and his children were stuck at home due to school closures and lockdowns. Later, I honed in on experiments done with very young children to try to find out how altruism develops. Research at the University of Washington showed that toddlers as young as about a year and a half will help an experimenter they believe needs their assistance.

Much earlier in my own life, a son who was then studying psychology in college urged me to check out the relatively new field of "positive psychology," focussing on what's right with us, rather than just diagnosing and treating what's wrong. At son Scott's suggestion, I read a pioneering volume, *Learned Optimism*, by Martin Seligman. Later I studied some of the work of the Hungarian-American psychologist with the difficult name, Mihaly Csikszentmihalyi. I read one of his seminal works, *Flow*.

Even earlier in my life, one summer at a family church camp I enrolled Scott as my assistant in the infant nursery. As the "baby of the family," our younger son had rarely gotten to care for children even younger than he was. His chance at about age four to be a "caring older brother" for a week was one of the highlights of his camp that year. It gave him a sense of power to be able to help care for the infants in the nursery. He was very caring, very careful.

It's important to me that the war in Ukraine end with as little additional carnage and displacement as possible. It's important to me that those whose lives and livelihoods were damaged by the war receive humanitarian assistance. It's important to me that those responsible for conducting the war be held accountable. It's important to me that we Americans find ways to reduce our epidemic of gun violence. It's important to me that we take additional individual and collective actions to reduce the future impacts of ongoing climate change and resultant catastrophic weather events. However, if I attempt to "fix" any of these issues by myself, I'm likely to get discouraged. All are big problems.

Instead of the "learned helplessness" of throwing up my hands or getting angry at slow-to-move officialdom or deciding that all these are somebody else's problems, I can practice learned helpfulness. I can pick and choose where my individual skills and actions would most likely make a positive difference and then use my skills, do the actions.

Like my four-year-old nursery assistant, I can engage in the "learned helpfulness" of altruism. I can make small but positive differences in the lives of those I interact with. I can continue to learn from my mistakes and improve. Learned help*ful*ness will glean better results than its opposite, I'm sure of it.

Chapter 24

Hallelujah Choruses

"Hallelujah, hallelujah, hallelujah, hallelujah, hallelujah."
                    —first line of Handel's "Hallelujah Chorus"

Handel's oratorio "The Messiah," and, in particular, its "Hallelujah Chorus," figures largely in our family's lore. Over the years, I've participated in several Handel Choirs, mostly as an alto. A vocal score of Messiah's choruses has somehow made it through our various moves. It sits, slightly musty, on a shelf in my office. Once covid concerns wane sufficiently, I hope to participate in future Messiah singalongs.

I'm not sure when I first heard this uplifting music, first performed in the mid-eighteenth century. Both my mother and her mother were practicing musicians, so it was probably early in my life. The first time I remember being fully aware of the majesty of the piece was the Christmas season I was ten years old.

Our immediate family's trajectory had been fairly typical of post-World War II small town America. My dad came home to Maryland from the Navy in early 1946, after serving on an aircraft carrier in the Pacific. He and my mom had married in 1944, during one of his earlier home leaves. After the war, they set up housekeeping in a one-bedroom cottage built by Mom's parents next door to their own house. Mom's parents wanted to keep their youngest close by, especially after their only other daughter and their one grandchild so far had moved cross-country to Seattle.

In 1947, I put in my appearance, followed in 1951 by a sister, then in 1953 by surprise twins—my youngest siblings, brothers to carry on the family name. Although Dad and some carpenter friends had added a second bedroom when my sister was born, it was tucked into an increasingly steep hillside. The slope precluded further expansion. Our small cottage was bursting at the seams. Dad and Mom were paying a minimal monthly rent to my grandparents, more as a sop to Dad's pride than anything approaching market rate.

Partly buoyed by this informal subsidy, by 1957 Dad and Mom had scrimped and saved enough to purchase a five acre piece of property about a mile away. Dad by then had become a small-scale residential construction contractor. He had the contacts and skills to be able to build his and Mom's dream house on the newly purchased land at minimal cost. They would start construction in March, 1958, once the ground thawed.

For our final Christmas at the cottage, we'd shoehorned into one corner of the living room a small fir tree with presents underneath. While we went next door for breakfast at Granny and Pop-Pop's, Santa would leave an even bigger pile of gifts to be opened after our return.

On prior Christmas mornings, we'd been awakened by Dad's best stentorian bellow: "Rise and shine, morning's a'wasting!"

This year was different. From somewhere near the stairwell leading from the living room to our basement-level kitchen, there was music. Every bit as loud as Dad, it had a decidedly different pitch and rhythm: "Hallelujah, hallelujah, hallelujah, hallelujah, hallelujah!" As we stumbled out of our bunk beds and wiped the sleepy sand from our eyes, we wondered what was producing the music. It didn't take us very long to locate the new walnut stereo cabinet with the record jacket to "The Messiah" placed carefully on top. Dad grinned at us, triumphant.

My father and my maternal grandmother had a respectful but sometimes strained relationship. Granny could be fussy about protocol and social niceties. Early in Dad's and Mom's married lives, before the arrival of children, Dad had gone out of his way one Christmas season to impress Granny. At considerable expense, he'd purchased three tickets to an evening performance of all three parts of Handel's Messiah in downtown Baltimore. He'd arranged transportation to and from the concert hall and had put on his one good suit to escort the ladies to this holiday tradition.

As retold at subsequent holiday gatherings, Dad was so tired after a busy day of physical work that he nodded off early in part one. When the "Hallelujah Chorus" began (at the end of part two), Dad startled awake. Most in the audience were getting up, a tradition supposedly started when, at the premier London performance in 1743, King George II had stood in homage to the "king of kings." Other audience members had followed suit. Standing for the Hallelujah Chorus became customary whenever and wherever the oratorio was performed. Dad wrongly assumed it was the end of the performance. He went to get Granny's and Mom's coats, much to Granny's chagrin.

Perhaps the 1957 hallelujahs were his way of celebrating the prospect of having a little more distance from his fussy mother-in-law. Perhaps he was just overjoyed at the prospect of a less crowded house.

After my dad's multiple careers were over, he developed dementia. For much of his decline, he was lovingly tended by my mom, assisted by a fairly robust social safety net that included veterans' benefits and a drop-in adult day care center. During his final few months, the burden of his care threatened to debilitate my mother as well. Our family reluctantly decided to put Dad in a nursing home. When my sister phoned to let me know that his body had finally died, she had the "Hallelujah Chorus" playing in the background. Somehow, it was a fitting testimony to Dad's release from suffering.

Many other "Hallelujah" choruses and anthems have been written, both before and since Handel's day. Given the fraught times we're living through, many of us may be drawn to the generally darker lyrics of a recent "Hallelujah" version by singer-songwriter Leonard Cohen. Cohen continued revising his lyrics almost up until his death in 2016. Despite multiple despondent verses, he nonetheless asserts in ending that he'll wind up singing "Hallelujah:"
...Yeah and even though it all went wrong
I'll stand right here before the Lord of Song
With nothing on my tongue but Hallelujah...
—Leonard Cohen, "Hallelujah"

I like to think that both Handel's and Cohen's "Hallelujahs" are relevant. We have suffered. We will suffer again. We have known joy. We will know joy again. Hallelujah!

About the Author

Jinny Batterson was born in Maryland just after the end of World War II. She grew up in a small town as a member of what came to be known as the "baby boom" generation. In adulthood, she has lived in Maryland, Virginia, Vermont, North Carolina and now California. She has traveled in all fifty states. For a total of about five pre-pandemic years, she lived intermittently outside the U.S., first in Canada, later in the small sub-Saharan African nation of Burundi (1983-85), most recently (between 2002 and 2012) in the People's Republic of China. Some of her prior essays and poems have appeared in regional and specialized publications. She contributed an extended essay to the collection *Writing After Retirement* (2014). In her 2017 memoir *Where the Great Wall Ends,* she chronicled her lifelong fascination and extensive travels in the big, diverse country that is China.

She's gradually adjusting to the generally mild climate of southern California and enjoys exploring the local sights.

www.ingramcontent.com/pod-product-compliance
Lightning Source LLC
Chambersburg PA
CBHW070643030426
42337CB00020B/4136